S0-CBX-864

*Limited Classical Reprint Library*

# Colossians

# A LETTER TO ASIA

BEING A PARAPHRASE AND BRIEF EXPOSITION OF THE EPISTLE OF PAUL THE APOSTLE TO THE BELIEVERS AT COLOSSÆ

BY

FREDERICK BROOKE WESTCOTT
D.D.

ARCHDEACON AND CANON OF NORWICH
CHAPLAIN-IN-ORDINARY TO H.M. THE KING

Foreword by
Dr. Cyril J. Barber

Klock & Klock Christian Publishers, Inc.
2527 GIRARD AVE. N.
MINNEAPOLIS, MINNESOTA 55411

Originally published by
MacMillian and Co., Limited
London
1914

Copy from the personal library of
Dr. Cyril J. Barber

0-86524-070-1

Printed by Klock & Klock in the U.S.A.
1981 Reprint

# FOREWORD

Benefitting from a singularly rich evangelical heritage. Dr. Frederick Brooke Westcott, son of the famous B. F. Westcott, followed in his father's footsteps by studying at Cambridge University and then entering the ministry of the Church of England. His first book entitled *St. Paul and Justification* was an exposition of the Apostle Paul's teaching in his Roman and Galatian letters. The *Cambridge Review* said of it:

> [Dr. Westcott's comments are] as we should expect, very much alive all through, and likely to be of great use as a text-book of scholarly method to that large, and sad to say rapidly growing class of students who come to the Greek Testament with very inadequate linguistic training. [His work] is at the same time full of suggestiveness for the maturest scholars. Above all, the writer's sense of the greatness and fascination of St. Paul cannot fail to impart itself as an inspiration to all who come within the range of his influence.

This same "suggestiveness" and "fascination" with the "greatness" of the Apostle's thought characterizes his exposition of Paul's epistle to the church at colossae.

Dr. Westcott's commentary, which bears the modest title *A Letter to Asia,* expounds the epistle with clarity and insight. His exegesis provides a solid basis for his comments on the text, and readers will find that he is more pastoral in his approach than was his illustrious father. The Greek text is quoted (for he wrote at a time when a high school education in England required a knowledge [though no longer a mastery] of Latin and Greek) and each citation is followed by the writer's own translation. The comments on the text are at once stimulating and relevant.

It is no wonder, therefore, that the TIMES of London, in reviewing Dr. Westcott's book, said:

> Students will be glad to make [his work] their guide in this impressive exposition of St. Paul's teaching . . .
> In both method and tone the book is a model of what New Testament study should be.

All things considered, this is a worthy publication and one which modern readers will enjoy for its intrinstic merit and value. I am glad that it is being made available again.

Dr. Cyril J. Barber
Author, *The Minister's Library*

# PREFACE

Some little time ago I put out a small work dealing with the doctrinal sections of Romans and Galatians. This was not unkindly reviewed by several public prints. Their words and the encouragement of friends, both known and unknown, determined me to go forward and deal with other Epistles as I had dealt with these. For various private reasons I first selected this one. The result is this little book. A formal edition it cannot claim to be. Years of study would be needed for the achieving of such a purpose. Nor indeed is it intended for the use of practised scholars. The people I have in my mind are those who still have time and energy for quiet Bible reading. I hope such will not be scared by the intrusion of Greek words. For more than forty years now I have been reading the New Testament in the original and, in common with many others, I think we have still a good deal to learn about its meaning.

For purposes of devotional reading I believe that the splendid version of 1611 will always stand. For private study, I think, something further is required in the way of a paraphrase or unfettered rendering. That I have made bold to supply.

If only any reader finds as much pleasure in the perusal of what I have written here as I have had in the writing, I shall be indeed much more than thankful.

And one word more I would say. To some it may appear I have dealt almost irreverently in one place or another with Bishop Lightfoot's famous name. May I say that his memory is dear to me, not only for his scholarship and his monumental learning, but also because I had in him the best and most generous of godfathers.

F. B. WESTCOTT.

NORWICH,
*January* 30, 1914.

# INTRODUCTION

When the writer of the Book of the Revelation sends greeting "to the seven Churches *which are in Asia*" the modern reader must remember that the name Asia does not mean in the least what it means now. 'Asia' in old days was no Continent, but only a single province—a large province, to be sure—in one region of the territories belonging to the Roman Empire. It was part of what we now call 'Turkey in Asia.' All the westward coasts of that land with a 'hinterland' stretching back for hundreds of miles in the shape of a long-sided, truncated triangle formed Roman 'Asia,' the Asia of St. Paul and of the New Testament writers generally. The 'Seven Churches,' all of them, lie in a comparatively small part of it. A triangle having a base one-third of the size of the other, and roughly proportionate to it, would cover all seven. Among them Ephesus has pride of place because it was the seat of government, and its position near the sea-board was central and commanding. From Ephesus, in Roman days, one main road led north-east in the direction of historic Sardis. Another crossed the mountains which lie to the south of the city, and took its downward way to the valley of Mæander. Its route thereafter lay due east along the valley. This was the principal road to the far east of the Empire in the days of Roman ascendancy; as it had been even earlier, thanks to natural advantages. It was, in fact, the 'Grand Trunk Road' from Ephesus to the the East, and that meant *from Rome to the East.* Through Magnesia, through Tralles, through Nysa it passed, and at intervals through other places less known to fame. At a distance of some hundred miles or so from the capital the river forks: that part which kept the old name flows to the north; the tributary flowing east and south is the historic river Lycus. This latter stream is of interest to us because hard by its banks lay three early 'Churches,' all mentioned in our Epistle—Colossæ, Laodicea, and Hierapolis. Imagine two sides of a square: that will give you three points, at the angle and at either end of the lines which form the angle. These three points will indicate the relative positions of the three well-known 'Lycus Churches.'

*Hierapolis* (a famous watering-place, and the mother of a famous son indeed, the philosopher-slave Epictetus) lay due north of Laodicea, a good way from the river and high above it; *Laodicea* nearer the river, but on the southern side of it, three miles or so away from it; *Colossæ* east of Laodicea with a touch of south, on the actual banks of the river, which divides the site in half. The main road made its way through Laodicea to reach Colossæ. Hierapolis stood upon another important road from the famous city of Sardis, making its junction with the great road actually in Laodicea. It follows that to pass from Colossæ to Hierapolis one would have had to journey through it. Of Colossæ even the site is not absolutely certain. Of Laodicea and Hierapolis there still are ample remains. Colossæ 'disappeared from history' in the seventh or eighth century. Its modern representative is a place called Chonas (anciently Chonæ) high up upon the slopes of Cadmus. In Saracenic days a situation on a main route was far too perilous. The old name 'Colossæ' was still retained for a time by titular Bishops who lived at Chonæ. But even that relic of the past was lost in the dismal course of the ninth century of our era.

Lying as it did, Colossæ was sure to play its part in the march of armies. Xerxes passed through it with his motley host marching westward; and the Greeks of the 'Anabasis' passed through it marching eastward. To this fact we are indebted for two early historical mentions. This is what the 'Father of History' has to tell us about it: 'Passing by a town of Phrygia called Anaua and a lake from which they get salt,[1] he came to *Colossæ* a great city of *Phrygia*, where the river Lycus tumbling into a chasm in the ground disappears, and then at an interval of some five furlongs reappears and discharges itself into the Maeander' (Herodotus vii. 30). About this we

[1] Professor Ramsay says: 'They still get salt from the lake as they did in Xerxes' days.'

can only say the river does not do so now. But it is a land of many earthquakes, and of a geological formation which easily lends itself to such phenomena.[1] However, the learned are not sure whether the statement of Herodotus should be accepted as true or not. Professor Ramsay thinks that Herodotus, who had never been there, is confusing two separate statements, one that 'within the very city . . . the Lycus enters a deep cleft in the ground'; the other that it 'issues from an underground channel and flows to the Mæander.' The 'real source' of the river (he says) is in the lake of Anaua, and the sound of a 'subterranean river' has been 'distinctly heard' at a point where part of its flow first 'issues from beneath the rock.'

This is Colossæ's earliest mention. It seems not at all unlikely that the name should be really 'Colassæ.' If so, it was possibly Herodotus himself who first changed the 'a' into 'o.' For '*colossus*' is a common Greek word, and 'Colossæ' would therefore sound far more natural to Greek ears than would 'Colassæ.'

And now for Xenophon's testimony. He tells us how Cyrus started from Sardis, marched through Lydia, crossed the Mæander on a bridge of seven boats, and so, after one 'stage' of marching, reached '*Colossæ, a habitable city, prosperous and large. There he stayed seven days*' (Anab. i. 2, 6).

I remember how eagerly a little boy, a great

[1] I am no geologist; but I think of the gorge at Meiringen and (still better) the gorge at Constantine in Algeria—both of them once complete natural tunnels.

many years ago, at his preparatory school, lit upon the familiar name amid the weary wilderness of 'stages' and 'parasangs.'

Colossæ, famous as it once was, owes all its glory now to the fact that Christ's Apostle was moved to write to the believers there a short letter of eighty-five verses, some six pages and a half of print. That letter, short as it is, has given the place addressed undying fame. We see, then, where they lived, these Colossian believers; in a town maybe still flourishing (though well on the downward grade as compared with its two sisters), lying on a great main road which led to the further East, and deriving (possibly) a respectable revenue from trade in wool. L. says it 'was without doubt the least important Church to which any Epistle of St. Paul was addressed.'

According to Ramsay, the proximity of its younger rival, Laodicea, upon the same main road and only eleven miles off, was fatal to its prosperity. The traffic of the road could not support both towns.

The flocks of the neighbourhood were famous both for the softness of their fleeces and for their aptitude for taking dye. The name *colossinus* was given to that particular tint which appears in cyclamen blossom. The sheep of Laodicea had natural 'glossy black' fleeces. The hue 'colossinus' (one would imagine) could hardly be undyed.

It is curious to think that although the town then lay on the very central route of traffic, commercial and other, St. Paul on his missionary journeyings had never passed that way (so far as we know). On his first tour he did not succeed in penetrating so far. On his second, had he had his own wish and not been "*forbidden to speak the word in Asia,*" he would naturally have travelled from Pisidian Antioch (which seemingly he did visit) through Celænæ and Colossæ *en route* for Ephesus. He did reach that great city on his return from Achaia (Corinth), but he arrived by sea, and by sea passed on to the port of Cæsarea, and so to his mission base in Syrian Antioch. When he visited Ephesus next, on the occasion of his long stay there, he came by another route than the valley one (*διελθόντα τὰ ἀνωτερικὰ μέρη*), as told in Acts xix. 1. Before his first imprisonment he never came there again; instead (as Acts xx. tells us), he sent from Miletus for the 'elders' of Ephesus and took solemn farewell of them, "*And now behold I know that you all, amongst whom I went about preaching the kingdom, shall see my face no more*" (Acts xx. 25).

How, then, did the Gospel come to the towns of the Lycus valley? That truly we do not know. All we can say about it is this, that in Acts xix. 10, we find the comprehensive statement, "And this continued for two years (*ἐγένετο ἐπὶ ἔτη δύο*) so that *all that dwelt in Asia* (*πάντας τοὺς κατοικοῦντεας τὴν* 'Ασίαν) heard the 'Word' of the Lord, both Jews and Greeks." Now, however much we may tone down this wide-embracing observation, it is plain that the phrase "*All Asia*" (if it has any meaning at all) could hardly exclude towns lying —and that, too, considerable towns—on the line of its main trade route and military road. We assume, then, with good reason that Colossæ and its neighbours were evangelised at that time; not by St. Paul himself, but by his active lieutenants (of whom he had good store) posting forward this way and that, while the master mind of all directed their operations from his headquarters in the capital. In Acts xix. we have four such active workers mentioned, Timothy and Erastus, "*two of them that served him as agents*," δύο τῶν διακονούντων αὐτῷ—where obviously there can be no mention of personal service; that is, of service rendered to the Apostle—in *v.* 22; and later on, Aristarchus and Gaius. Any one or all of these may well have helped in the work. Timothy, indeed, almost certainly did; else why should he be mentioned by St. Paul in the opening of the Epistle? But if Timothy bore some part in the work of evangelisation, it plainly was not the chief part. For that is definitely assigned to another, to *Epaphras* in *v.* 7 of chapter i. This Epaphras was with St. Paul at the time of writing. His greetings are sent in the letter. Of his zeal for his own converts iv. 12, 13 vividly testify; as does the earlier chapter of his faithful discharge of the work of instruction in the Truth.

But where was the letter written, and when, and why?

We know the circumstances which called forth the letter. That question is easily answered. Where it was written and in what year are harder matters to settle.

The Apostle, *in prison* somewhere, had met with two Colossians. One was Epaphras, their evangelist. He had told his famous chief of the 'Christian love' which ruled in the Church of the far-off city (Col. i. 8). At the same time he had also evinced a singular anxiety as to the condition of the believers there. What caused this anxiety we can only find for ourselves from the perusal of the letter. But of course it would be *error*, in one form or another—error in faith, or error in practice. Lightfoot holds that 'we may suppose he came to Rome for the express purpose of laying this state of things before the Apostle.'

The other visitor, when he came across the Apostle, was not concerned at all about the Colossian Church or any of its troubles. He was merely a runaway slave, oddly named *Onesimus* (in English 'helpful' or 'profitable'), who had possibly hoped to bury himself and conceal his identity—as evildoers still do—amid all the throng and turmoil of the imperial metropolis. Rome, moreover (if we believe the Roman satirist), was ever the happy hunting-ground of all Greek-speaking adventurers. A good deal of responsible work was done in ancient days by persons of 'slave' status. Accordingly Onesimus, though he may have been a rogue when he ran away from Colossæ, was probably in addition a person of some capacity. Indeed his successful flight would plainly suggest as much. His master was *Philemon*, no doubt a prominent member of the little community of believers at Colossæ. How this slave, with the common slave name, found his way to acquaintance with the prisoner Apostle we cannot tell. But he did, and was won by him for his Master, Christ (" *my child, Onesimus, whom I have begotten in my bonds,*" Philem. 10), and became from love and gratitude his very dear and 'helpful' attendant. Yet he had, in all Christian honesty, to make amends to the 'master' whom he had wickedly defrauded of a chattel in himself. And so he must be sent back to the old slave life in Asia. His part in the writing of the Colossian letter is limited to this: that his affectionate presence constituted one more tie between the Apostle in prison and the Church he "*had never seen*" in the far-off Asian city (Col. ii. 1). There was then an occasion for writing, and a messenger ready to face the long and wearisome journey. Not that Onesimus bore the letter. For *Tychicus* (it is supposed, and very naturally) went with him charged with that. The two believers travelled together, the freeman and the slave, entrusted alike with the duty of giving all the news of the famous prisoner to the anxious 'brethren' and 'children' in the Asiatic Province.

But *where* was the prisoner prisoned? That is a question upon which 'doctors' have 'differed,' and will differ.

We possess four 'prison letters'—Philippians, Ephesians, Colossians and Philemon. (2 Timothy, another 'prison letter,' in any case belongs to a different period.) In each of the four letters we come across plain reference to the writer's circumstances (see Phil. i. 13, 14, 17; Col. iv. 18;

Philem. 10, 13; Ephes. iii. 1, and iv. 1). It is usually thought that some interval of time separates the three latter letters from the former. The question that divides the opinions of the learned is this: Was Philippians written before the three, or was it written after? Lightfoot maintains the former hypothesis; the more part of modern writers appear to incline to the latter.

But, granted there was an imprisonment so long in its duration that the Apostle was able to achieve (in spite of it, or thanks to it) a considerable success in making known the Gospel (see Phil. i. 12 and following), and friends in far-off Philippi thought it worth while to send him all that way a welcome contribution (Phil. iv. 10, ff.); are we to identify this imprisonment with either of those that are mentioned in the Acts? Is it the imprisonment at Cæsarea (Acts xxiv. 27), or the imprisonment at Rome with which that book concludes (Acts xxviii. 30, 31), or is it yet a third? I merely mention a third because a modern writer postulates an imprisonment at Ephesus, to which may be 'partly assigned' the 'prison letters' (Deissmann, *St. Paul*, p. 16). Whether his suggestion will carry conviction, I cannot tell. But old-fashioned folks will probably be content to make their choice between Cæsarea and the Roman capital. For me, I hold to Rome. The '*prætorium*' view of Lightfoot still counts with me; the view that that word implies 'the prætorian guard' at Rome (Phil. i. 13), as our Revised Version takes it. Rome also seems to me a far more likely place for purposes of communication with Macedonia and Asian 'Churches' than Cæsarea could be. Moreover, why should Onesimus make his way to Cæsarea? There was every possible reason why he should wish to go to Rome, as the safest of all hiding-places. If any should be inclined to urge that Rome was a long way to go, I would venture to reply that we must neither exaggerate the length of the journey nor disparage the energy of the travellers of those days. There is extant the record of a merchant who travelled some fifty times between Rome and the Province of Asia. Clearly they thought little enough of the distance.

The *date* goes with the place. If it be Rome, it will be two years later; if Cæsarea, two years earlier; and, on the whole, one would incline to the view that more of time would suit the general conditions better. Still there cannot be any certainty upon such a question as this.

And now, we must bear in mind that the letter *is a letter*. The realisation of this simple truth is one of the greatest gains of the last few years, largely due to the discovery that in form and in language and everything (except, of course, their religious aspect and all that carries with it) St. Paul's letters *are as others. They are not formal treatises.* It follows that to analyse them as if they were must be (if one views things sanely) somewhat misdirected zeal. In pursuance of this belief, I am proposing next to supply not a formal analysis of the letter to Colossæ, but merely an informal abstract. I intend to reproduce in modern form and language the general drift of it. After that we will discuss some questions suggested by the letter, more particularly the question as to the nature of the error which so disturbed Epaphras and (presumably, on his report) his chief, the great Apostle.

Here is the substance of the letter, somewhat shortened and modernised.

### An Abstract of the Letter

**The Address.**

To the 'Church' at Colossæ Paul and Timothy send all Christian greeting.

**The writer's thankfulness.**

What I hear of your faith and your love and of your clinging to the great Hope, which is yours in the Gospel —your Gospel and all the world's—fills me with thankfulness. It has been so with you, ever since you learned from Epaphras the true story of God's Grace.

**His prayer for them.**

It is Epaphras who has told me of your love. I pray unceasingly for your growth in Christian knowledge and your advance in Christian life. I would have you strengthened by grace in courage and patience and joy; always rendering thanks to God for calling you to your share in the saints' inheritance; for rescuing you from darkness and bringing you into the Kingdom of His Son, our Redeemer, our one source of Forgiveness.

(*His position is unique.*)

**Christ's supremacy in creation and in the Church**

*In Him* is revealed to us the very nature of God. In Him all things created, whether seen or unseen, by what name soever called, have their existence. He is creation's beginning and its end. And, as it is with creation, so is it with the Church. The Church is the Body, He the Head. As in the resurrection, so everywhere, *He is first* . . . He is supreme. For why? In

Him the 'Plenitude' of the Godhead was pleased to take up His dwelling, and in His Person to achieve a perfect reconciliation of all that is to God. The 'blood of the Cross' has achieved it. To you too estranged and enemies of God in the bad old heathen days, this reconciliation extends. You shall be presented before Him holy and blameless entirely, provided you loyally stand by the truth of the Faith; provided you do not *let yourselves be moved* from the Gospel—the world-wide Gospel, the Gospel you were taught, the Gospel that I preach.

based upon His Godhead,

which has enabled Him to achieve a reconciliation,

which is theirs as it is others'.

I am glad of all I have to bear; I am glad to suffer as Christ did, on behalf of His Body, the Church. For God has allowed me to be His minister in this matter, to preach the wonderful truth so long concealed, but now revealed to men in all its splendour—the truth, *which is Christ.* Him I would proclaim with all my might. '*In Him*' I would have all 'perfect.' To that end I toil and strive, and He works with me.

To preach Christ is his dear privilege.

I am very anxious for you and for the Laodiceans and all the Churches that are unknown to me personally. I would have them full of love and full of wisdom. Above all I would have them know Christ. *To know Him is to know all.* Don't be misled by any. Christ is everything. I rejoice you are firm in the faith. I am with you in your efforts to be firm, though far away. Stand, I say, by the old teaching. There are folks who talk big and high about 'Philosophy.' Believe me, it is all delusion. It is all human imagining, all frankly unspiritual. Once again, Christ is wholly God: your one hope rests in Him. He is above and beyond all '*powers*': His is the only '*circumcision.*' His death you share by baptism, and His new risen life. You, I say, are 'raised' by faith. Dead you were, but now are alive. Your sins are all forgiven. By means of the cross He has triumphed over all ill powers that are, and stripped them of their glory.

He would have them (and all) understand Him.

Christ is everything.

Let them cling to that truth!

Let them not be led astray by talk about 'powers,' about 'circumcision.'

Theirs is a new life.

Rules and regulations have no life-giving force.

Mind not then about trifles. Regulations as to eating and drinking and feasts and sabbaths are only 'shadow': Christ is the 'Substance.' Don't yield to those who would overpower you with strange ideas of *bowing to angels*. It may seem humility, but is really mere vain imagining.

Union with Christ ensures all.

Christ (once more) is the Head. Connexion and contact with Him assure both grace and growth.

Away with false asceticism!

They must live 'in heaven.'

Union with Christ implies death to all trivial regulations. Eschew, then, all vain asceticism. For all its seeming reasonableness it leads to nothing. Your thoughts should be set above. Where Christ is, there is the seat of your own life (for all you may not realise it). When He is fully revealed, you shall share His glory. But, if your life be in heaven, you must have done with things of earth. The old heathen sins must go; sins of flesh, sins of wrong desire, sins of temper, sins of bearing, sins of falsity. Put off the old self, put on the new—which is ever *being renewed* until we fully know Him. In Him all distinctions vanish, and He is simply All.

Give up the old life; live the new,

with all its characteristic marks.

Yours, then, must be His virtues; compassion, humility, gentleness, a readiness to forgive. Above all you must have love. Without love is no perfectness.

Let Christ's Peace rule in you. Be thankful. Dwell on the thought of Christ: endeavour to understand Him. Auspicate all you say or do with His great Name.

Counsels for all 'sorts and conditions.'

Wives, be submissive. Husbands, be loving. Children, be obedient. Parents, be patient. Slaves, obey your earthly masters and do your very best, for Christ is your real Master. And He is yours too, masters; so be just and fair to your slaves.

Pray with all your might: remember me in your prayers: ask that I may have opportunity to deliver my message and use it boldly.

Be very careful of your conduct before the heathen world.

Tychicus and Onesimus will tell you all about me.

His messengers will tell all about him.

Aristarchus and Mark and Jesus Justus (those loyal Jewish Christians) all salute you. If Mark comes, welcome him.

Epaphras too sends greeting. He is very anxious about you; you are constantly in his prayers.

Various brethren send greetings.

Luke too and Demas send greeting.

Greet the Laodicean Church: greet Nymphas.

Let them greet neighbours from him, and read this letter and the other.

Let this letter be read aloud in Colossæ and Laodicea. Read *their* letter too.

Tell Archippus to be diligent in his office.

Note my sign manual.

Autograph farewell.

Remember me in my prison.

God be with you.

A rapid perusal of the letter will show how very hard the first part of it is, and how simple by comparison is the other. The main gist of it plainly is the *all-importance of Christ*, as Way and Truth and Life. But a good many of the sentences are very hard and obscure.

It is far from easy to be sure exactly what false teaching had obscured the Central Figure of our Faith. One thing only is plain enough, that the writer has not in his mind such a detailed and clearly articulated 'Gnostic' system as was imagined by expositors of a generation since. There is nothing in the letter which cannot well belong to the age of the Apostle. The word *pleroma* itself, which excited so much suspicion, is used in a natural sense and not a technical one. It cannot in all fairness be taken as an indication that the letter emanates from the days of developed

Gnosticism; the days of the wild and extravagant systems identified with such names as Basilides and Valentinus. From whatever the 'Church' in the letter was suffering, it was not suffering from a full-fledged 'Gnosticism.' Nowadays no one imagines it. One thing alone stands out as abundantly clear. The root of the trouble lay in this, that somehow the position of Christ, in creation, in redemption, in life-giving power (both here and also hereafter) had been disparaged. Other elements had been intruded as necessary factors in vital Christianity. *His All-sufficiency* had been disputed. It was not now as it had been at the date of the four great Epistles, a question of Christianity pure and simple, as distinguished from Christianity engrafted upon Judaism; so that Circumcision and the Law were regarded as indispensable even for Gentile converts. Things had gone much further than that. The trouble was more complex, though probably not nearly as complex as would appear from the perusal of Lightfoot's famous dissertation.

Turn we then to the Epistle and endeavour to detect indications that may guide us to the nature of the difficulty. That the 'truth of the Gospel' was threatened appears from the second paragraph (i. 6, 7); that the Apostle detected in them an insufficient appreciation of what Christ means for the Christian is plain from i. 9. In *v.* 14 follows an assertion of His relation to our redemption, to our forgiveness of sins. These things (they are really one), we are told, we have "*in Him.*" Upon this statement there follows a Christological passage of very great intricacy, containing puzzling terms such as *eikon* and *prototokos*, as to which we well may doubt whether we have mastered yet their full significance. But, in any case, Christ is put forward as possessing a unique relation to all that may be called 'creation.' All of it came into existence (ἐκτίσθη) "*in Him.*" Next, 'all creation' is divided by a double classification. Things may be regarded as 'things of heaven' or 'things of earth'; or again, as 'things visible' and 'things invisible.' At this point are introduced certain very significant terms, 'thrones,' 'lordships,' 'rules,' 'dominions.' Whatever these things be, the Apostle declares they are all in every way subordinate to Him. In relation to their existence, He is efficient cause; He is also final cause. Over them He possesses, from every point of view, an absolute '*priority.*' But what are they, these shadowy entities? The words are plainly technical terms, but technical terms from where?

The answer would seem to be supplied by one of those many writings of Jewish origin, but non-canonical, to which the attention of scholars has lately been so much directed. In the *Book of Enoch*, in a section which is assigned by Dr. Charles, the master in this kind, to the years 94–79 B.C., we read the following:

'And he will summon all the host of the heavens, and all the holy ones above, and the host of God, the Cherubim, Seraphim, and Ophannin, and all the *angels of power*, and all the *angels of principalities*, and the Elect

One' (a designation of Messiah), 'and the other *powers* on the earth and over the water.'

(*Book of Enoch*, lxi. 10, Dr Charles' translation.)

This section unhappily does not exist in Greek. But, even apart from that, we cannot avoid being struck by the similarity of language. 'Powers' and 'Principalities' are indubitably terms derived from the later development of Jewish 'angelology.' In the text of our Epistle they must be mentioned *with intention.* A doctrine of 'angels' was clearly one of the disturbing influences at work in the little Colossian body. Clearly also 'angels' somehow were represented as having a part in the achieving of human redemption, which St. Paul could not allow. These are only created things, and He is not. He is GOD—it is here we meet the mysterious terms of i. 19—and, because He is God, is all-sufficient 'Redeemer.' In *v.* 23, further down, the Apostle urges them, with a passionate earnestness, not to yield one inch on this point.

So far we have detected one element of error—a usurpation of the place which should be Christ's alone in the minds of the Colossians by certain 'angelic' beings.[1] What part they were thought to play, these 'powers' and 'principalities,' in man's spiritual emancipation, I cannot tell. But we seem to have here the germ (a 'Judaistic' germ) of the later Gnostic dogma of 'emanations'

[1] It is of much interest to note that even till much later days the Archangel Michael was Patron Saint of Colossæ (and of Chonæ). A magnificent Church, which bore his name, existed for many centuries, till destroyed by Mohammedans.

or 'æons,' invented to bridge the gulf between God and man—that 'gulf' for which Christ alone is the only conceivable Bridge (see St. John i. 51).

In the later section of chapter i. (*vv.* 24-29), we have no further light thrown upon the 'Colossian Heresy,' as it is called. There is merely a further insistence upon Christ as the very heart of the Christian revelation. The exact drift of *v.* 27 is not very easy to grasp, but it would seem to consist in this, that Christ is man's one Hope, and that further this hope is extended to the hitherto excluded Gentile. In *v.* 20 one may detect a not very obvious reference to a '*wisdom*' that was abroad, the work of the false teachers who troubled the Asian Church.

The same word 'wisdom' (σοφία), now coupled with 'knowledge' (γνῶσις), reappears in the next chapter (ii. 3), where we are told decisively that "*the stores of wisdom and knowledge*" are all "*hidden away*" in Christ. This also seems to point to an esoteric doctrine, repudiated by St. Paul with all his energy, that was now in vogue at Colossæ. He admits its plausibility (ii. 4), but fiercely denies its truth. To dally with such figments is a mere *desertion* of Christ. So we should gather from *v.* 5, if we read between the lines.

The warning of ii. 4 is reiterated in ii. 8. But now it begins to take a more palpable form. The false teaching (whatever it was) was designated by its followers as a *philosophia.* But it presents itself to the writer as virtually tantamount to a repudiation of Christ, and as being merely 'human,' at once in its origin and also in its development. On the one hand it is purely fantastic, on the other it is purely material—of the earth, wholly 'earthy.' Christ in impressive contrast stands forth as a Being Divine. Verses 9 and 10 are very hard and baffle the commentator. They do not correspondingly trouble the ordinary reader. He sees that their teaching is, *Because Christ is God, therefore He can fully satisfy all human aspiration.* His ability to do so depends on What He Is.

At this point we are face to face with another Colossian error. This time it is an old enemy. There were clearly folks at Colossæ who (after Galatian models) were calling out for circumcision, were raising once more the banner of the 'Judaistic' revolters. To this literal 'circumcision' the Apostle opposes the spiritual (ii. 11), and passes on to expound the whole doctrine of the 'new life'—the life which has its beginning in the cancelling of sin. Here again (for one little moment) the "*powers*" and "*principalities*" reappear (ii. 15). But mark a curious difference. Last time we came across them they were apparently beneficent angelic powers, apprehended as discharging a function more properly belonging to the Christ. How are they represented now? They are "*triumphed over*" by Christ; they are "*paraded*" as His prisoners; they are "*stripped*" of all their spoil (or of all their armour). Are we then to conceive that they are no longer 'angels of good,' but 'evil angels'? It seems a sudden and a violent change. Or is this Triumph of Christ, achieved through the Cross, merely a figurative way of saying that by His transcendent sacrifice He proved Himself to be—to the exclusion of all other beings that might conceivably be imagined to have part or lot in the matter—the sole and only Redeemer of Mankind and of all Creation? This idea I put forward with considerable hesitation (it has not, so far as I know, been suggested by others). Without some explanation the introduction of 'evil powers' seems too abrupt. If 'evil powers' they be, these 'rules' and 'dominions' here (and, of course, in Ephes. vi. 12 such ill powers do occur as the foes we have to meet), they cease at once to have any sort of connexion whatever with the heresy of Colossæ. *They are the writer's, not his opponents'.*

The next verse, in any case, tells us more about wrongful teachings then current in the Church. The Colossians are solemnly warned against letting any take them to task in regard to certain particular observances and practices—of eating and drinking, to wit; and of keeping of holy days, feasts, new-moons, sabbaths. They are reminded that all this is merely 'shadow.' Now all the regulations suggested by these terms (in spite of the mention of 'drinking'; for there was the Nazirite law) might well be Judaistic. But it is not easy to read any normal Judaism into what follows immediately after. The verse is indeed obscure, but at least its meaning is not suggestive of the views and practices we associate with Israel. They are bidden not to be "*overruled*" by persons who should insist on "*worship paid to angels*" in a spirit of *lowliness.* It is true that Deissmann has seen in this merely reference to '*the Law*'; the 'angels' who were present at the Giving of the Law (see Gal. iii. 19) being taken to represent it in such sort, that he who bows to the Law may be said to "*worship angels.*" But I cannot say this seems to me a convincing theory. It seems to me far more likely that the 'angels' here must stand for spiritual intermediaries between God and man. But if the view which identifies the 'Angels' with the 'Law' does not greatly commend itself, what are we to say of that other, which detects in the following phrase a definite reference to heathen 'mysteries'? What have 'angels' to do with 'mysteries'? And yet there must be some link between the two clauses. If the very puzzling expression "*standing on* (?) *what he has seen*" means 'taking his stand upon the mysteries in which he has been initiated'—and this, I apprehend, is what Professor Ramsay suggests—how in the world are we to harmonise it with the words that go just before? Is it not a far safer course to suppose that the whole of the sentence has to do with the 'angel-intermediary' notion, and either to suppose that the text is here disturbed by primitive corruption, or boldly to adopt the inserted negative and render "*dwelling on things he has never seen*"? At any rate, if we do so, the whole sentence hangs together, and that is very much. It is not that St. Paul disbelieves in the existence of angelic beings. With the words of Christ in his mind he never could do that. But he does disbelieve in the rôle which is thrust upon such 'creatures' by what he characterises as mere human imaginings (read carefully ii. 18). Such notions are doubtless clever. What puts them 'out of court' altogether, in the Apostle's estimation, is simply this—that they are not true and are not Christianity.

In all this, then, we merely return to the false doctrine hinted at in i. 16—the doctrine that lesser beings are to be taken into account by man in seeking reconciliation and communion with the Deity.

On the speculative side, then, the Colossian error would seem to have all been centred in this—the degradation of God's Christ by the gratuitous interpolation of other 'intermediaries' between Creation and the Creator.

But there was a practical error.

This plainly took the form of a rigorous asceticism. Rules and regulations were plainly multiplied; not the rules of orthodox Judaism, but of a something which went much further. It probably included (see ii. 21) abstinence from marriage, vegetarianism and total abstinence (in the modern use of the phrase). Now all these practices obtained amongst a sect of Jewish mystics called the Essenes. Judaism, it would seem, was always apt when brought into close contact with other oriental faiths to take into itself these curious religious ideas, which have ever had so much vogue in the mysterious Orient; above all, the belief that *matter* is the source of all evil, and that, consequently, the *body* is the enemy of the *soul*. This doctrine plainly leads to two corollaries: one, that the soul only is immortal; the other, that the body must be rigorously subdued by unceasing discipline. The Essenes superadded to an ultra-strict observance of the ancient Law of Moses at once that dualism involved in the tenet that evil has its primal source in matter; and also its concomitant, the practice of an exceedingly austere asceticism. Besides being 'sabbatarians' of the most marked character, they were also opposed to marriage. L. quotes from Josephus a passage which says, 'Marriage was viewed with suspicion by them . . . they shrank from the contact with women; moreover they disbelieved in woman's fidelity.' They were strict vegetarians too; they would not touch oil or wine. In a word, they were 'ascetics' through and through. Moreover (and this is deeply interesting), upon the dogmatic side they seem to have set great store on the activities of *angels*. L. quotes from Josephus the kind of 'terrifying' oath the Essenes took: they swore 'they would have no secrets from their brothers, and would reveal none to any one else; that they would transmit no doctrine whatever in a garbled form; that they would refrain from robbery, and jealously guard alike the sacred books of their sect and *the names of the angels*.' Now to what intent should a man preserve so solemnly secret the 'names of the angels,' unless somehow they were to be used in something of the nature of magical incantation?

It would seem, then, as if the erroneous teachings at Colossæ which troubled Epaphras so could all of them be traced to a *Jewish* origin. Angelology played a large part in later Judaism. Also (as we have seen) an un-Mosaic asceticism was found among certain sectaries.

*In these two* primarily consisted the Colossian 'heresy.' On the one hand, they vainly supposed that other beings could aid in their redemption; on the other, that the path of bodily 'mortification' is the way that leads man to God. Against both of these errors alike St. Paul sets Christ.

The danger of a false asceticism appears again in 1 Timothy. There (in chapter iv. 3) the Apostolic writer decisively condemns vegetarianism and the like (of course, in so far as they are regarded as absolute essentials to any truly religious life); and abstinence from marriage, commended on similar grounds. At the close of the same epistle he has a word of warning against *gnosis,* that is, 'esoteric' tenets, such as are definitely hinted at in such a verse as ii. 18.

Phrygia, it is perfectly true, was 'Orient of the Orient' and (no doubt) a perfect hotbed of fantastic religious ideas. And Colossæ was in Phrygia, though included politically in the province of Asia. Yet I do not think we need look to any purely 'heathen' source for the mistaken beliefs entertained by the little Christian community. Too much has been made of them. The famous Essay of Bishop Lightfoot is a marvel of erudition, but it invests the Colossian trouble with a complexity which one would think can hardly belong to it.

The origin of the 'angel' idea one would like to know more about. But unhappily it is here that information fails us. We can only build up hypotheses on what we learn from Apocryphal books, and upon the tantalising hint which Josephus' statement gives us.

Only a very short word is needed as to the genuineness of the Epistle. The earliest reference (a wholly undoubted one, 'we were taught that Christ is the firstborn of God' . . . 'we have recognised Him as the firstborn of God and before all creatures') is found in Justin Martyr (A.D. 100 – *circ.* 160). It is included in the Epistles catalogued in the Muratorian Fragment (*circ.* 170); it was included in certain ancient Versions. Only on purely 'subjective' grounds is its authenticity disputed. Again, interpolations have been imagined; but it is hard to make any theory of such interpolations square with the phenomena of our MSS.

As for the style, it is excellent 'Pauline,' of a very convincing character. When we read Ephesians and Colossians side by side, we feel inclined to say that if we had to choose between them (on the theory that one or other of the two could not be genuine) we should certainly take Colossians. On the other hand, Ephesians is very much better attested. Internal evidence claims the one as genuine, external claims the other. We had better accept them both without demur. At least the writer of either did not 'copy' the other. The curious little divergences make that impossible.

# THE TEXT OF THE EPISTLE

## CHAPTER I

THE Letter, following the normal type, opens with a sentence which tells us who the writer is and who are the persons addressed. Such a sentence (though, to be sure, the tone in a Pauline letter is of necessity somewhat more solemn than in more trivial correspondence) really answers in effect to the common modern form, 'My dear So-and-so, I hope you are very well.' It is important to realise that these 'letters' really are 'letters,' and nothing else. The rich discoveries of ancient ephemeral correspondence, that have come to light in the last few years, have placed this beyond all dispute. Again and again, when we read them, we are positively startled by the closeness of the likeness which obtains between these treasured letters of the Apostle and those of ordinary people in his day. Our letter then opens thus·

i. 1, 2. "Paul by divine 'will' an 'apostle' of Christ Jesus and Timothy the 'brother' to the 'saints' that are in Colossæ—I mean the faithful brothers 'in

Christ'; grace be to you and peace from God our Father."

There is little here which calls for comment. Remember, as you read, which other letters belong to the same period as this; to wit, Philippians, Ephesians, and Philemon. The order of their writing is a matter of much dispute. Thirty years since Philippians was put first, and the other three (including this one) at a later period close together. Nowadays Philippians is placed last. Anon the pendulum will swing in the old direction. Anyhow Colossians and Philemon were written together and sent together. Ephesians (see above), being a 'circular' letter to several Churches, was penned at much the same time, though it did not reach Colossæ till it had been to Laodicea. Timothy is not coupled with the Apostle in the Ephesian salutation: he is in Philippians and, of course, in Philemon.

St. Paul here designates himself "*an apostle . . . by divine will.*" With regard to 'will' it should be remembered that the word is decisively concrete. Paul is an 'Apostle' because God would have it so, in His Mercy and His Goodness. The phrase is not intended to emphasise the writer's personal merit, as Lightfoot very justly observes. 'Apostle' is a term of exceeding interest. One would say, after consideration of textual phenomena, that the written Gospel contained this statement about the Twelve, "*whom also He called Apostles.*" All Editors read it in St. Luke, vi. 13; some in St. Mark, iii. 14. It looks as though it should be regarded as original in the latter. Three chapters further on we read (vi. 30), "*and the Apostles gather themselves together unto Jesus.*" Plainly the words 'the Apostles' become rather inexplicable, if one extrudes the earlier mention of the name; especially in view of the fact that nowhere else in St. Mark, and only once in St. Matthew (x. 2), and never in St. John, are the Twelve so called. Once, indeed, in St. John the word does occur, but not as a technical title (xiii. 16). It is, for the most part, 'Lucano-Pauline.' Hebrews has it once, *but used of Christ Himself*; 1 Peter has it once ("*Peter an apostle of Jesus Christ,*" i. 1); Revelation has it three times. In xxi. 14 we have "*the twelve Names of the twelve Apostles of the Lamb.*" In xviii. 20 we have (in Pauline manner) 'Apostles' and 'Prophets' coupled together. Rev. ii. 2 would seem to speak of 'Apostles' other than the Twelve. It is always possible that in such a passage as this last it would be better not to render 'Apostle' at all, but rather 'messenger.' It is the 'My' which bears the emphasis in this place, not the 'Apostles.'

When St. Paul speaks of himself as he does here we cannot mistake his meaning. 'Apostle' means, for him, one directly commissioned by Christ (as it were, a *legatus* of Christ). The supreme dignity of the office thus denoted is declared by the words which follow, "*by Divine Will.*" It is well known (at least, I suppose, it is generally admitted) that the writer uses the term both in a 'high' sense and in a 'low' one. In the 'low' sense it might be applied (though I do not think it is, as a matter of fact) to such as Timothy. Timothy (as in 2 Corinthians) must be content to rank as a 'private' in Christ's Army. Paul stands on a different footing altogether. He claims to be no whit inferior in 'status' to the Twelve. An individual Christian is styled "*brother.*" Collectively 'believers' are (in the later Epistle) denominated "*saints.*" In all Epistles, from Romans onwards, the address runs "*to the saints,*" instead of "*to the Church.*" It is generally supposed that in his later days a growing sense of the oneness of the Church made the Apostolic writer increasingly unwilling to retain his earlier phraseology. In this case we must notice that all the 'saints' are not of necessity 'loyal' or 'faithful' brethren. Their adherence may be only nominal. At all times the Church on earth contains both good and bad. At Colossæ (as we shall see) some had drifted, or were drifting, from the simplicity of the Gospel. There was heresy afoot, and those who were misled by it are carefully excluded by the limiting phrase "*and loyal brethren in Christ.*" Whether the ἐν Χριστῷ should be attached to the whole of the phrase, or only to the latter clause, is precisely one of those questions which each will decide for himself. A good deal can be said in support of either alternative. I myself incline to the latter, because I think that the solemn formula "*in Christ,*" strictly speaking, cannot apply to any but those who may rank as members of the Church Invisible.

"*Grace be to you and peace*" is the invariable

greeting in all the Pauline letters till we reach the Pastorals. Sometimes (as in 1 Thessalonians, the earliest letter of all) it stands unsupported; here we have "*from God our Father*"; more commonly it runs (as in 2 Thessalonians) "*from God the Father and the Lord Jesus Christ*"—a form in that early connexion of singular significance. As for the terms 'grace' and 'peace,' it will be enough to say that the addition of the former decisively 'Christianises' the traditional greeting of Israel. It makes it plain what sort of 'peace' the writer has in mind; and further, how it comes. The real 'peace' belongs to those on whom rests the 'favour' of God. 'Grace' is (of course) a most complex term, but I think that, in such usages, the sense is as here indicated.

Pauline letters (and herein we gather they did not depart from contemporary models) generally have immediately after their opening 'salutation' some pious expression of 'thanksgiving.' In this our Epistle is normal. The paragraph of thanksgiving, without being quite as complex as that in the sister Epistle, exhibits a similar tendency to 'roll on' from point to point as ever new ideas occur to the writer.

i. 3, 4. "On every occasion, when I pray for you, I thank the Divine Father of Our Lord Jesus Christ, because I have heard tell of your faith † as Christian men † and your love towards all the saints. . . ."

A great deal of uncertainty besets the rendering of these apparently simple words. To begin with, there is the plural *εὐχαριστοῦμεν.* I translate that, without hesitation, '*I* thank,' because I feel perfectly certain it is not Paul *and Timothy* that we must think of here, but only Paul himself. For me it is indisputable (in spite of all old prejudice) that the Apostle did speak of himself in the plural, whenever he chose to. Next, the expression "*the Divine Father*" (*τῷ θεῷ πατρί*) is absolutely unique. The Greek is odd—in effect, untranslatable. But the Editors are clear about it; and probably it should stand. *Πάντοτε περὶ ὑμῶν προσευχόμενοι* would seem to mean "*on every occasion, when I am praying for you,*" that is, 'whenever my prayers include you.' The participle *ἀκούσαντες* ("*because I have been told of*") gives the reason for this constant thankfulness. But what is it (we wonder) that the Apostle has been told of them, in his far-off prison-house? Look at the words dispassionately and you might be inclined to think that the Colossians displayed two excellent virtues; "*loyalty*" (*πίστις*) to their Master, and "*love*" towards all the brethren; towards the Church and all its members not only at Colossæ, but wherever it existed. The question is, Can we extract this sense from the former clause? I have marked the dubious words, in the paraphrase above, with a double obelus. "*Your faith in Christ Jesus*" might obviously mean "the faith you have, which comes to you *through Christ Jesus.*" Or it may mean, "the faith, which you have, being Christians." It cannot mean "your belief in Christ Jesus"; that is, Jesus Christ cannot possibly be the object of the 'faith.' In itself the word πίστις can mean either 'faith' or 'faithfulness.' We clearly are not helped to a definite decision by the knowledge that τὴν πίστιν ὑμῶν ἐν Χριστῷ Ἰησοῦ is 'Pauline' for τὴν πίστιν ὑμῶν τὴν ἐν Χριστῷ Ἰησοῦ. Or, rather, we may say that in Classical Greek we might either read in this place τὴν πίστιν τὴν or τὴν πίστιν τῶν. That is, the article to be supplied might belong to πίστιν, or belong to ὑμῶν. To say (with L.) that 'the preposition denotes the sphere in which their faith moves' is to say nothing intelligible.

What one desires to know is, how we are to paraphrase the original words in Greek to exhibit the thought beneath them. I should say, the sense probably is τὴν πίστιν ὑμῶν (τῶν) ἐν Χριστῷ Ἰησοῦ ὄντων. That is why I would paraphrase "your faith" (or, "your loyalty"—I don't know which) "*as Christian men.*" In this case we have to sacrifice the antithesis suggested above. But that may easily go. It is unusual in St. Paul to meet a complete antithesis. Accordingly, for two things the Apostle is thanking God. The believers at Colossæ (or some of them) had 'faith,' or 'faithfulness'—a matter for sincere thanksgiving: they also had 'love,' and a love of a far-reaching kind. It extended to 'all the saints.' Whether ἣν ἔχετε should be read or no (after τὴν ἀγάπην) appears to me to be of very slight importance. It does not touch the sense either way.

Perhaps, seeing we have here the whole of the three great virtues which form the familiar triad, we had better keep 'faith,' not 'faithfulness';

for if 'hope,' the abstract virtue, does not follow, it does come in a concrete form. This calls to mind the passage in 1 Thess. i. where we find the three Christian graces named (with a somewhat difficult phraseology) in the same order we have here — faith . . . love . . . hope. There faith 'operates' (shall we say?); love 'toils'; hope 'endures,' or 'holds fast.' It is 'hope' that ministers courage and keeps up 'faith' and 'love.' So is it here. They 'believe' with Christian belief; they 'love' with Christian love of the very broadest kind; precisely because they have 'hope,' or rather a definite hope.

Διὰ τὴν ἐλπίδα κ.τ.λ. must be joined to the words that precede more immediately. It does not 'throw back' to εὐχαριστοῦμεν. The Christian Hope (as I have said) makes all things attainable. All things are possible *for him who hopes.*

i. 5-8. ". . . because of the Hope which is laid up for you in the heavens; of which you were told long since by the message of the true Gospel; which has come to you, as it also is all the world over; bearing fruit and ever extending—as it also does in you, since the day that you were told of it, and came to know the Grace of God, as it really is; as you learned from Epaphras, our beloved fellowservant, who is on my behalf a faithful minister of God's Christ; who also has showed me how you love as spiritual folks should."

There is nothing in all this particularly difficult. The Christian 'hope' is mentioned again in *v.* 23 below; less distinctly in *v.* 27. The phrase ἐν λόγῳ (which, of course, suggests preaching) τῆς ἀληθείας τοῦ εὐαγγελίου reminds us of Galatians. There is only one genuine Gospel. That is why the writer is not content to say simply 'the message of the Gospel.' Twice in this one paragraph the word *truth* occurs. This we see to be only natural, when we remember that the Gospel had been improved upon at Colossæ, and had lost its old simplicity beneath a cloud of new ideas. Τοῦ παρόντος εἰς ὑμᾶς explains itself. After ἐστίν, I think, should be a comma. Ἐν παντὶ τῷ κοσμῷ implies that there are some Christians everywhere. Καρποφορούμενον καὶ αὐξανόμενον brings forward a new conception. Not only does the Gospel 'exist' everywhere; it is everywhere producing its inevitable results, 'beautiful lives' (καρποφορούμενον), 'expanding influence' (αὐξανό-μενον). Where the Gospel is, moral beauty is; where moral beauty is, adherents follow. All missionaries know that! It was at Colossæ as everywhere else. They too knew the Gospel power, the Gospel's compelling influence. From the very first—from the day when they first heard and "*got to know*" (not, "*knew fully*") the truth about God's great goodness, His 'undeserved favour' (χάριν), it always had been so. The paragraph ends with a well-deserved compliment to the faithful teacher who had brought the Gospel to them. Whatever errors there were at Colossæ the fault did not lie with Epaphras. Him he calls his 'fellowservant' (a term only here, in St. Paul, and in iv. 7). Further, he speaks of him as 'Christ's Minister in his (St. Paul's) stead.' Ὑπὲρ ἡμῶν makes better sense—provided we are ready to believe that it can stand for St. Paul alone. For me, I believe it can. What St. Paul himself could not do, this loyal man had done. He had preached; and had preached the truth. Nor had his services (as towards the Apostle) ended there. He had visited him in Rome with news of the Church's state. It was from him St. Paul had learned of the 'love' that was in the Church, marking it as a real Church, of 'spiritual' persons—persons living *in the spirit.* Τὴν ὑμῶν ἀγάπην ἐν πνεύματι is another of those expressions which the translator must expand as best he may. In this case we suppose that the 'Spirit' (or is it the 'spirit'?) brings the love. Where the Spirit is, love must be.

i. 9, 10. "For this cause I too, since I was told, have not ceased praying for you and making supplication, to the intent you may be filled with the fuller knowledge of His will and be altogether wise and spiritually understanding; that your walk may be worthy of the Lord in all subservience; and may bear fruit in every good doing, and that you may grow through growing knowledge of God. . . ."

The 'for this cause' in this section may be very perfectly illustrated from 1 Thess. ii. 13 and Ephes. i. 15. The latter is a particularly close parallel. In such a case it is not easy to be certain what the words mean. It is just the kind of phrase which the writer uses vaguely. Here we gather in a general way that the report of their spiritual progress stimulated his intercession.

Because they had gone so far, he would have them go even further. The correspondence between ἀφ' ἧς ἡμέρας ἠκούσατε ('from the day when you were told') and ἀφ' ἧς ἡμέρας ἠκούσαμεν ('from the day when I was told') I believe to be merely accidental. There is no real antithesis. In fact the statement in the clause does not mean precisely the same in the two places. In the latter it is more literally true. From the very moment he received the report of Epaphras the Apostle's zeal in prayer was actually redoubled. The middle voice of the verb *αἰτεῖν* (in so far as it differs from the active) we may assume to deepen the sense of personal interest. That is, in effect, *αἰτεῖσθαι* is stronger than *αἰτεῖν*. The clause ἵνα πληρωθῆτε κ.τ.λ. ('to the intent ye may be filled') is, of course, a defining clause: it gives us the scope of the prayer, and not its object. The construction is singular. So far as I can see, there is no complete parallel. The passive of the verb πληροῦν ('fill') is usually associated with the genitive case of the thing with which the 'filling' is. Possibly the peculiar phrase in Ephes. i. 23 may exhibit a partially similar accusative. However, there πληρουμένου is more likely to be 'middle.'[1]

As for ἐπίγνωσις itself, it would seem to mean not 'recognition' (as it frequently does) but 'further' knowledge—'additional' knowledge. By derivation (plainly) it might easily mean this. 'Perfect' knowledge goes too far. A consideration of the well-known verses in 1 Cor. ii. (*vv.* 7, 8)

[1] The Dean of Wells, I see, regards it as passive.

will suggest that Christian σοφία consists primarily in this: a knowledge or apprehension of the Divine Will—*God's 'Will' in creation.* To know that is to know all, for in it is contained the answer to Life's great riddle. This is of all the Whys, which set men thinking, the one great and central 'Why.'

The words which follow are an expansion following a common 'Pauline' form. That is why I venture to paraphrase by means of independent clauses. Bishop Lightfoot bids us observe that the σοφία and σύνεσις we find here, coupled with the φρόνησις, which takes the place of our σύνεσις in Ephes. i. 8, make up the Aristotelian triad of intellectual virtues. Of these three σοφία ('Wisdom') is the highest; σύνεσις ('understanding') is critical; φρόνησις (generally rendered 'prudence'—a poor sort of thing!) is essentially practical. In Ephesians (*l.c.*) the 'all' is attached to the 'wisdom' and the 'practical judgment' (φρόνησις); taken in close combination, as the results of the apprehension of the "*secret of His Will*" (τὸ μυστήριον τοῦ θελήματος αὐτοῦ). It is interesting indeed that St. Paul should chance to employ, in these parallel sentences, the phraseology of Aristotle. But I doubt whether Aristotle was consciously in his mind. I feel pretty certain he wasn't. On the contrary, I should hold that the καί in Ephesians is merely 'and,' whereas here, in Colossians, it is a καί of 'identity.' 'Spiritual discernment' (or 'understanding') constitutes what St. Paul calls 'wisdom.' The Greek terms 'wise' and 'wisdom' are necessarily employed in many different senses. 'Wise' (σοφός) may mean 'cultured' or 'clever' or really 'wise.' It follows it may denote a 'wisdom' which is none (as in St. Matthew xi. 25, "the wise and understanding"), or a 'Wisdom' which is genuine to the very highest degree. Such a religious, spiritual wisdom the Apostle craves for his converts.

To pass on, it is curious that both here and in Ephesians (iv. 1) we have ἀξίως περιπατῆσαι, where one would have anticipated περιπατεῖν. The aorist presumably regards the 'walk' as whole and one. This I have tried to express in my paraphrase ("*that your walk may be worthy*"). In Ephesians he urges them to "*walk worthily of the calling wherewith they were called*"; in 1 Thessalonians—how interesting it is to note in that earliest Epistle very nearly the same phrasing as in these late ones—we have "*to walk and to please God*" (περιπατεῖν καὶ ἀρέσκειν Θεῷ); here it is "*worthily of the Lord*," undoubtedly meaning Christ. The word I have rendered 'subservience' has an interest of its own. In Greek moralists it bears an evil sense: it is the unwholesome complaisance with which flatterers and courtiers approach an earthly potentate, to his great hurt. 'Towards the King of kings' (as L. happily says) 'no obsequiousness can be excessive.' His colon after ἀρέσκειαν commends itself to the judgment. Καρποφοροῦντες ('bearing fruit') and αὐξανόμενοι ('growing') are grammatically 'irrational.' In spite of their irregular case (for they should by rights be accusative) they undoubtedly refer to the subject of περιπατῆσαι, that is, to the Colossian believers. The "*further knowledge of God*" (τῇ ἐπιγνώσει τοῦ Θεοῦ) may express that in which the Apostle prays that his readers may develop, or that which will lead inevitably to moral growth and consequent 'fruitfulness.' We may render either "grow *through* growing knowledge," or "grow *in* growing knowledge." The former appears the likelier.

Two more participles (also in the nominative) carry us forward in the next two verses. They virtually represent new petitions in the Apostolic prayer. Let us render them accordingly.

i. 11, 12. ". . . That you be empowered with all power, after His all-glorious, conquering might, so as to be altogether brave and altogether patient—aye, and joyful too! Giving thanks to the Great Father, that hath made us believers fit for a share in the lot of the Saints, that stand in Light."

The various Greek terms for 'power,' 'might,' and the like, are discriminated by commentators. One of the two that here occur, the second (the word κράτος), belongs by N.T. usage to God alone. It means essentially 'the power which prevails.' The phrase is further heightened by the addition of τῆς δόξης αὐτοῦ. The 'He'—as it must for Christians — refers to the Christian's Master. Further, we should note in passing that 'power' (δύναμις) is the Pentecostal term. Of ὑπομονή and μακροθυμία it may be safely said that the former is not 'patience' (it is 'fortitude,' a grander thing), while the latter is a part of it. It is that kind of 'patience' which calmly bears ill-usage. The mention of 'joy' (μετὰ χαρᾶς) is a point of contact with Philippians. Every student will remember how in that Pæan of the Prison-house the Apostle dwells upon the supreme duty of joyfulness; will recall the pious Bengel's characterisation of the Epistle in his famous epigram, "*Summa epistolae, gaudeo, gaudete.*"

If ἡμᾶς be rightly read in *v.* 12 it covers the Apostle, his readers, and all Christians: it is an 'us' of the most comprehensive. For πατρί some read Θεῷ—a variant of no importance. The verb ἱκανοῦν (to 'fit') recalls 2 Corinthians iii. The two words μερίς ('share') and κλῆρος ('lot') are virtually synonyms. The rendering may be 'our share in the lot,' or 'the share, the lot' (an appositional phrase)—"*who hath fitted us for the portion, the lot of the Saints.*" Ἐν τῷ φωτί may represent "that is in Light," or "that are in Light." An article of some case and gender must be mentally supplied. 'Light' is the believer's 'inheritance'; the conception of 'inheritance' coming, of course, from O.T. times. L. compares the well-known words of St. Paul in Acts xxvi. They illustrate not only the φῶς, but also the further phrase as to the κλῆρος of the saints:

"... unto whom I send thee"

(it is the Great Missionary's commission from his new Master),

"... for to open their eyes,
that they may turn from darkness to light,
and from the reign of Satan unto God,

> that they may receive remission of sins
> and a lot amongst the sanctified
> (κλῆρον ἐν τοῖς ἡγιασμένοις)
> through faith in Me."
>
> (Acts xxvi. 17, 18.)

The Hymns of Zacharias and of Simeon in St. Luke i. ii. will naturally occur to the mind in connexion with the thought of Light.

The verses that follow next after have also their connexion with the passage just quoted from Acts.

i. 13, 14. "Who has rescued us from the reign of darkness" (ἐξουσίας τοῦ σκότους recalling the "reign of Satan" above) ". . . and has transferred us to the Kingdom of the Son of His love; in Whom we have our redemption, the remission of our sins."

No doubt in these two verses the writer of set purpose contrasts the *ἐξουσία* of darkness with the *βασιλεία* of the Son, but it is not needful to say (with L.) that the word *ἐξουσία* may stand for tyranny. Indeed his own instances do not bear it out. The term is a neutral one. The character of the dominion, or domination, depends on the ruling power. Our Old Testament story will illustrate the force of the "*has transferred.*" Wholesale removals of populations were common with Oriental potentates. The verb is, however, not technical. L. bids us remark that the language employed by the Apostle implies that 'the reign of Christ is already begun': further, that he loves to dwell on the potentiality of salvation. Of the Church it is true she is 'saved'; she is 'redeemed';

she has entered into 'the Kingdom.' There were Christians at Colossæ of whom these tremendous things could hardly be affirmed. 'Redemption' (ἀπολύτρωσις), to judge from O.T. usage, means 'deliverance' pure and simple: there is no thought of 'ransom' in it, in spite of all appearances. The language of Ephesians must be compared with this:

> ". . . His grace wherewith He graced us
> in the Beloved
> (ἐν τῷ ἠγαπημένῳ),
> in Whom we have our redemption
> (ἐν ᾧ ἔχομεν τὴν ἀπολύτρωσιν)
> by means of His blood,
> the remission of our transgressions."
> (Ephes. i. 7, 8.)

Whether there be aught in L.'s idea of some false teaching about 'redemption' in vogue in the Asiatic Churches, which the Apostle desires to controvert by defining Christian 'deliverance' as he does, and identifying it distinctly with 'remission of transgressions,' I cannot tell. (See his note on p. 143.) 'Redemption' is not in St. Paul by any means a common expression, and even where it is found it sometimes has reference to the future and final redemption—in fact, I believe more often than not in his few usages. They are only seven in all. It cannot surprise us then if here (as in Romans iii. 24) he explains what he means by the word, that there may be no mistake, quite apart from any question of false teaching at Colossæ and in 'Asia' on this head.

Meanwhile the solemn phrase "*the Son of His Love*" has prepared and paved the way for a Christological statement of the most important kind. It follows without pause or break, and teems with technical terms calling for careful, if brief, discussion. "*Who is the* image *of the invisible God*": so runs our familiar version. But what is meant by *image*? What lies behind it? How shall we give it a meaning which will speak to the plain person?

To begin with, let this be said. In later Judaism there came a growing sense (to put the thing very plainly) of the very tremendous gulf which separates God from man. Hence not only did that anthropomorphism, which we can trace in the early scriptures, recede into the background. More than that, first 'Wisdom' appears in the Scriptural books as the 'reflection' or effulgence (ἀπαύγασμα) of the Deity, and the 'image' (εἰκών) of His goodness; and then in the Alexandrian School the 'Logos' doctrine takes shape. God is 'the Absolute.' The 'Logos' is His *manifestation* in Creation and all that follows on the first creative act. ('Logos,' of course, in English 'word,' covers both 'word' and 'thought.') Now the 'Logos' in Philo is called, not once only but many times over, the 'image' (εἰκών) of God. But mark this! The Philonian 'Logos,' though He be the 'image' of God, is Himself *invisible* (ἀόρατος). The Incarnation for Christian believers has wholly altered this. St. John's λόγος 'σὰρξ ἐγένετο.' In short, Christ, the Incarnate Son, is the veritable 'image' of God—of God invisible; whereas the Philonian 'Logos' (so far as man is concerned) is but a shadowy entity. The thought of Him does not help matters. The Incarnation does. It is indeed an effective bridge to cross that unimagined chasm which parts man from his Creator. When Philo denominated his 'Logos' (or Word) the 'image' of the Eternal, he meant that He was like God, a true representation of God, cognisable by the mind, in some degree—which obviously God is not. As Plato conceived that man by a process of pure reason might ascend to the realisation of the very 'idea' of Good, the 'actual Good' itself; so (presumably) the Alexandrian sage conceived of the possibility of apprehending intellectually the Being of the Word. As for 'image' (εἰκών) itself, the word implies definite 'likeness.' The εἰκών of a thing reproduces it distinctly upon the mind, or the eye. Our 'Word,' the Word of St. John, is indeed the εἰκών of God. The true meaning of the Pauline phrase is given us by these statements from his Gospel:

> "God no one hath ever seen"

(here we have the "*God Invisible*" of our text);

> "the only begotten Son"

(is the right reading Υἱός or Θεός? the context suggests the former),

> ". . . Who is in the bosom of the Father"

(cf. the first verse of the Gospel),

> ". . . He hath declared Him";

(St. John i. 18.)

and

"... he that hath seen ME hath seen the Father; how sayest thou, Show us the Father?"

(St. John xiv. 9, 10.)

Strictly speaking, 'image' implies not only 'likeness,' but 'visible likeness.' Shall we then make bold to start with this audacious paraphrase?

i. 15. "Who is the Visible Likeness of God Invisible."

Theologically it is true; although we must remember that, wholly apart from the Incarnation, the Eternal Son remains *εἰκών*. He is *εἰκὼν Θεοῦ* eternally. The element of 'manifestation' (which L. properly argues is included in the term) came *for us*, when He came on earth—when "*the Word—became—Flesh.*"

The language of Heb. i. 3 must naturally be compared.

Then follows another phrase, about which it would be easy to multiply words indefinitely. That is, *πρωτότοκος πάσης κτίσεως*, in our Version "*the firstborn of all creation*" (R.V.). This is open to misunderstanding, for (supposing it to be correct) it conveys, to English ears and English minds, the idea that somehow or other He, the Son, is part of creation. No doubt it is not meant to; yet indubitably it does! Now Philo's 'Logos,' once again, was described by a Greek term very closely resembling "*firstborn.*" Philo styled Him not *πρωτότοκος* but rather *πρωτόγονος*. Further he spoke of the Logos as the 'eldest son' of God. Between Philo's term and St. Paul's it is hard to draw any distinction. One means 'firstborn,' the other 'firstbegotten.' Difference really there is none. St. Paul employs the term he does because it carries with it Old Testament associations. 'The firstborn' (L. says) became a title of Messiah. It carries with it the idea of primogeniture; and from that follows in natural sequence the conception of ownership—yes, even of sovereignty. It follows that the phrase "*firstborn of all creation*" might suggest to the reader the notion 'heir of all creation.' Really two ideas should be in it: first the priority of the Son to any creation; next the heirship of the Son over all created things. Regarded merely as *Greek* the word would mean (I think) "*begotten before all creation.*" This L. dismisses as 'unduly straining the grammar.' Yet the phrase he quotes himself (from St. John i. 15, *ὅτι πρῶτός μου ἦν*) seems to bear out such a rendering.

In the end we have to choose between "*Creation's firstborn heir*" and the version just given. Which is it to be? My mind inclines to the latter. It is just a question whether the stress in the following words lies on the thought of 'sovereignty' or on that of 'priority.' Who shall decide? But maybe the time has come when we may venture on a continuous paraphrase.

i. 15, 16. ". . . Who is the manifest Likeness of God invisible; begotten before all Creation (or, possibly, before all the Creation); for in Him were all things created, in heaven and upon earth; things visible and things invisible; whether 'thrones,' whether 'lordships,' whether 'dominions,' whether 'rules'—all things created are through Him, and unto Him. . . ."

Here 'all things' (τὰ πάντα) is all-inclusive. It is the same doctrine as the Johannine:

"All things came into being through Him:<br>
and apart from Him came into being<br>
no single thing,<br>
which is in being. . . ."<br>
(πάντα δι' αὐτοῦ ἐγένετο· καὶ χωρὶς αὐτοῦ ἐγένετο οὐδὲ ἕν, ὃ γέγονεν.) (St. John i. 3.)

There the "*no single thing*" exactly answers to the "*all things*" here. The article makes not much difference, in accordance with Pauline usage.

The preposition employed to express this creative energy of the Son is hard of explanation. The Philonian 'Word' and His activity—one feels almost tempted to say 'its' activity rather than 'His'—is normally represented either by διά ('through') with the genitive—which implies an 'agency'—or even by the 'instrumental' case, the dative. This latter enables us to estimate the immense distinction between the Alexandrian and the Christian 'Logos.' Here, however, we do not find the διά we expect, the διά of personal agency, which we find at the close of the verse. In its place we have an ἐν. Ἐν αὐτῷ ἐκτίσθη τὰ πάντα: so it says. There is a similar ἐν in St. Paul's speech on Mars' Hill (Acts xvii. 28). But there the reference is not the same. St. Paul is speaking of God Himself, not of the Son as such. And I think we may safely say that the ἐν in relation to the Father (the source and fountain-head of Deity) is more easily intelligible than in relation to the Son. Anyhow it suggests to the mind a certain flavour of pantheism. For this ἐν must clearly be discriminated from that 'instrumental' ἐν we find in later Greek not uncommonly. Of that we can be certain. The instrumental ἐν reveals itself by the nature of the noun that goes with it. That noun should not be a person. Hence we are perfectly safe in concluding that the ἐν is here employed as implying rather more than the usual διά of agency. In effect, *it covers both the διά and the εἰς which come below.* Both 'agency' and 'end' are included in it. Creation and all it involves is represented as centred in the Person of the Son. We recall the χωρὶς αὐτοῦ ('*apart from Him*') of St. John—χωρὶς αὐτοῦ οὐδὲ ἕν. Whether the definite article be read, or no, with ἐν τοῖς οὐρανοῖς and ἐπὶ τῆς γῆς (that is, whether we are to read "*in heaven and on earth,*" or "*things in heaven and things on earth*") is a matter of small importance. The two phrases used by the writer expand in two directions the "*all things*" that precedes them: 'heavenly things, earthly things'; 'visible things, invisible things.' Let there be no mistake about it! Regard all things (excluding, of course, the Deity Himself) from any point of view you will, and the solemn fact remains. The existence of everything that is depends upon the Son. At Colossæ, as we have seen, a mistaken reverence had interposed between God and Man a chain of subordinate beings, called generically 'Angels.' Into the *arcana* of these speculations the Apostle does not choose to pry. It is enough for him that the believers at Colossæ have been caught in the specious net. As to the exact details of the teaching which had misled them he remains stedfastly incurious. The very way in which he mentions the mystic jargon of the Angelologists makes the thing abundantly clear. He seems to say in contempt: Call those fancied beings what you will! It is all one to me! In fact, in the corresponding passage of the Ephesian Epistle (Ephes. i. 21) he does not even employ the same denominations, in speaking of these phantasies. There he asserts of the Son, that God has exalted Him

"... above all rule and dominion and power and lordship and every name that is named" (every 'title' that is 'respected') "not only in this world (*αἰῶνι*) but also in the world to come."

The 'thrones' in that place disappear, and another term ('powers') is employed, which is not found here. However, there he clearly has in view not only the shadowy powers of imagined 'angelic' beings, but also substantial 'powers'—such powers as we have on earth. All authority, earthly and other, is wholly subordinate to the authority of the Son. Here, I think, the 'thrones' and 'lordships,' and all the other terms, apply only to mystic beings, such as the Asiatic heresiarchs were fain to whisper about. For the rest, we can find all the terms employed here and in Ephesians in contemporary writers (see L.'s note). In Colossians they are mentioned—it may only be accidental—in descending order of dignity. Those who were conversant with such speculations regularly placed 'thrones' and 'lordships' first. At least, so it would appear. The Apostle did not, of course, disbelieve in angelic beings, but he did oppose most strenuously the idea that any such beings could in any way 'mediate,' as between God and His Creation; could in any way interfere with the prerogative of the Son. So far as they had 'being' (and the angelic hierarchy, of which folks talked in Colossæ in esoteric circles, were mainly mere creations of a fevered imagination) they owed everything to Him. And so we come once again to the old decisive pronouncement (now stated in a new form) "*Everything is created by Him and (everything) unto Him.*"

There is no tense, be it observed, in N.T. Greek which is so baffling to the translator as the perfect passive is. "*All things . . . have been created*" will not, really and truly, suffice. We need an expanded paraphrase to set forth all the Greek says. For the Greek perfect is not a 'past' tense, as the English perfect is. It is actually 'perfect': that is, it represents a fact *which is now*, though it has its roots in the past (whether that past be near or remote).

'Everything that is in being owes its creation to Him: everything which is in being has its final cause in Him.' All that is comprehended in this dictum.

A statement closely akin to this in our text is found in Romans (xi. 36). There it is said of God "*for of Him* (*ἐξ αὐτοῦ*) *and through Him* (*δι' αὐτοῦ*) *and unto Him* (*εἰς αὐτόν*) *are all things.*" There, you will see, a preposition the Apostle mostly employs in speaking of the Son is employed of the Father—I am speaking of the *δι' αὐτοῦ*. Here, on the contrary, we find an *εἰς αὐτόν* ("*unto Him*") which we should naturally expect to refer to the Eternal Father. See the doctrine as fully expounded in 1 Cor. xv. 28.

> ". . . But when the day shall come, that all things shall be subjected unto Him" (It is implied we cannot tell when that time shall be. But somehow, somewhere, the prophecy of the Psalmist of long ago shall have its complete fulfilling—such a fulfilling as the singer never imagined), "then shall the Son Himself be subjected to Him that shall have subjected all things to Him THAT GOD MAY BE ALL IN ALL."

Here, and in Ephes. i. 10, we do not carry our thoughts to the last great stage of all, the supremest consummation, the "*subjection*" of the Son. Seeing that the dignity of the Son is in dispute, we concentrate our minds on the last great stage but one. Accordingly, here we read Τὰ πάντα . . . εἰς αὐτὸν ἔκτισται ("*all things exist with Him as end*"); while there the same truth is figured in another most arresting form:

> ". . . according to His 'good purpose' which He proposed to Himself, in Him"

(ἣν προέθετο ἐν αὐτῷ).

". . . (a purpose) to be worked out when the full time should have come"

(εἰς οἰκονομίαν τοῦ πληρώματος τῶν καιρῶν; the εἰς here is 'temporal' and means 'against').

". . . to 'sum up' all things in the Christ. . . ."

(ἀνακεφαλαιώσασθαι τὰ πάντα ἐν τῷ Χριστῷ).

(Ephes. i. 10.)

Broadly speaking, GOD is the END, the one great END of all. Yet is His Eternal Purpose achieved 'in' and 'through' the Son.

i. 17. "And HE IS before all things and everything that is owes its mode of existence to Him."

For this αὐτὸς ἔστιν ("*He is*") L. very justly compares the 'I AM' of Exodus iii. and the ἐγὼ εἰμί of St. John. The "*is*" (do not fail to note) is idiomatic Greek. *We* should be tempted to say "*He was*" (just as in St. John viii. 58). In Greek one does not say, 'I have been waiting long,' but 'I am waiting long.' The present tense covers both; all the waiting that has gone and the waiting that still is. In the same sort of way this "is" covers all the interminable past as well as the unending present. It is the right and proper tense to set forth eternity of being. "*Before all things*" is palpably right. But the 'all' of the original is indeterminate in gender. Hence the strange Latin mistranslation of the Vulgate: *Ipse est ante omnes.* The Greek preposition might stand for superiority of rank, not priority in time. But such a rendering is exceedingly unlikely. Moreover, as L. points out, πρό would not be the normal preposition for expressing such a truth in 'Pauline.'

No! it is forceful reiteration of what has been said before, a restatement of the truth in πρωτότοκος πάσης κτίσεως. "*And in Him all things consist*" (τὰ πάντα ἐν αὐτῷ συνέστηκεν) is a highly noteworthy phrase. R.V. margin says, 'that is, hold together.' But, I should say, it is more than that. Philo (as L. bids us mark) spoke of the 'Logos' as the 'tie' or 'bond' (δεσμός) of all Creation. So under συνέστηκεν lies the derivative σύστασις. Things are, and remain as they are, because of the Son.

Verses 15-17, then, have set forth with imposing force the position of the Son in regard to all Creation. His position and authority, in regard to all that is, are entirely unique. Now the reader must contemplate His relation to the Church. As with the Primal Creation, so is it with the New Creation—what we might call the Re-Creation. Here, again, there is one great term to describe His supreme position. Πρωτότοκος πάσης κτίσεως He was, and is, above; that is, "*begotten before all Creation.*" Now He presents Himself as πρωτότοκος ἐκ νεκρῶν ("*firstbegotten from the dead*"). The repetition of the old term perhaps suggests that the leading sense of the word is rather 'priority' than 'heirship.' The Apostolic writer is in no way bound in such matters. He might use 'firstbegotten' once with a stress on the thought of primogeniture, and again immediately after with no such stress. There is an instance of this fluidity before our very eyes. The *αὐτός ἐστιν* of *v.* 18 is wholly different from the *αὐτὸς ἔστιν* of *v.* 17. Yet outwardly the words are just the same. They only differ in accent, that is, in intonation. Yet the one stands for 'HE IS' (with all its tremendous associations, in Old Testament and in New), while the other is merely 'He is,' or, possibly more correctly, '*He* is.'

i. 18. ". . . And He is the 'Head' of the Body, the Church; seeing He[1] is its source and beginning, first-begotten from the dead, that everywhere He may prove in Himself pre-eminent."

Let us first discuss this "*Head.*" In the Gospels we have the word only once in a figurative sense. That is in the Lord's own quotation from the Psalm (St. Mark xii. 10 and parallels), "*the stone which the builders rejected, He has become the Head of the Corner*" (*οὗτος ἐγενήθη εἰς κεφαλὴν γωνίας*). Whether this well-known citation had any connexion with the later N.T. language about "*the Head*" it is difficult to say. 'Head' reappears in a figurative sense in 1 Cor. xi. and xii. Christ is the 'head' of the man, and the man is the 'head' of the woman (1 Cor. xi. 3): God, too, is the 'Head' of Christ. Chapter xii. contains the parable of the 'body' and the 'members.' There the body, as a whole, is identified with Christ. The 'head' is only one member with the rest of them (see *v.* 21. "*The eye cannot say to the hand . . . or again the head to the feet, I have no need of you*").

[1] (ὅς apparently equivalent to ὅς γε.)

The Church is merely 'the Body.' The conception of a 'headship' is not yet. That comes in this group of Epistles. Indeed, it is nowhere else. We have it in Ephes. i. 22. "*He appointed Him supreme Head of the Church, seeing it is* (ἥτις ἐστί) *His Body* (?)"—whereupon there follows that phrase so inconceivably baffling, τὸ πλήρωμα τοῦ τὰ πάντα ἐν πᾶσιν πληρουμένου; from out of the mist of which emerges the great truth that somehow He is not 'complete' without His Church, to minister to that 'completeness'; and yet to be 'full,' 'complete,' is the very nature of Him. We have it again in iv. 15, where of Him it is simply said, "*Who is the Head.*" Yet again, in v. 23, we have a recurrence to the figure of 1 Cor., the thought of man as the 'head' of the woman, as Christ is the 'Head' of the Church. In Colossians we have it here, and in chapter ii. 10 (not in relation to the Church, but to all authority whatsoever), and in ii. 19 ("*not holding fast the Head*"). The teaching of the group is plainly 'mystical.' The 'Head' metaphor does not exhaust the whole relation of Christ to His Holy Church. It merely states one side of it. The head is no longer regarded as part of the body. It is ἀρχή in every sense: it is 'source' of the body's vitality; it is the seat of the body's governance. I call the teaching 'mystical' because (as I apprehend) it regards the Eternal Son as being simultaneously 'in' the Church, and also 'outside' it.

Ἀρχή ('beginning') is a wonderful term, with

a great intellectual history and a singular range of meaning. Systematic Greek thinking began with it. The original Asiatic 'hylozoists' starting by asserting that this, or that, was the ἀρχή of all things. With them ἀρχή meant the 'principle' to which the underlying unity of the visible world of things might be attributed. A certain solemnity cannot but attach to the word from these associations. In regard to its use in N.T., this may well be said. In the Gospels it is only found in a temporal sense, often in adverbial phrases, such as 'in the beginning' or 'from the beginning.' There is, of course, the transcendental ἐν ἀρχῇ ("*in the beginning*") of St. John i. 1, 2. That is peculiar to himself and stands alone. In 1 John it only appears in the formula ἀπ' ἀρχῆς. In the earlier Pauline letters (Rom., 1 Cor.) it stands only for 'rule,' 'authority.' In Ephesians it occurs in no other sense than this. Here only in Colossians does it represent 'beginning.' The purely 'temporal' sense we detect in Pauline writings only once (Phil. iv. 15). An ἀρχή which illustrates this of Col. i. 18 can be found in Revelation. There not only have we the statement (in chapters xxi. and xxii.) that HE is the 'Alpha' and the 'Omega,' the "*beginning*" and the "*end*," but it is also said of Him (and that, mark, in the 'letter' to the Church at Laodicea) that He is "*the beginning of the creation of God*" (ἡ ἀρχὴ τῆς κτίσεως τοῦ Θεοῦ). That phrase does not correspond with the phrase before us now. Rather it answers closely to our earlier πρωτότοκος ("*firstbegotten of all creation*"). This ἀρχή primarily has reference to the 'spiritual' Creation, the second Creation, which we have called the Re-Creation, the Birth of the Church. And possibly (let us only say, 'possibly') the immediate neighbourhood of πρωτότοκος here suggests that we should read into it, of the word's three principal meanings, viz. priority, origin, authority, the second rather than the third, the first rather than the second. Let us say that κεφαλή safeguards the thought of 'rule,' while ἀρχή puts before us the idea of what we might call 'first'-ness. Plainly, however, the 'source' conception (which may only be traced, notwithstanding, in Rev. iii.; if indeed it be there) need not be wholly excluded. For the ἀρχή before us here is a something larger and wider than the ἀπαρχή (a word which bears a strictly limited sense) of 1 Corinthians xv. That is 'firstfruit': this is more. (Why L. feels called upon to explain the absence of the definite article with ἀρχή, I cannot at all understand. Surely, it is rather its presence which would have called for apology.)

In Rev. i. 5 Jesus Christ is called ὁ πρωτότοκος τῶν νεκρῶν ("*the firstbegotten of the dead*"). The phrase marks the reality of His death. Here I should say His description as the 'firstbegotten' —that is, the "*firstborn*" in the New Creation— must not be taken to imply that He shares in the 'new' Creation, that *He* was 'dead' as men are 'dead'; I mean, *spiritually* dead. We were 'dead' and have been given 'life.' He is the life. I say this because it is borne in on my mind that ἐκ τῶν νεκρῶν (from its very form) suggests rather the death of figure than the death of fact. But others may not think so, and may see a complete correspondence between this phrase of Colossians and the phrase in Revelation.

But let us pass on to the end of this very fruitful verse.

We have already paraphrased the clause which completes it in the following terms: "*that everywhere He may prove, in Himself, pre-eminent.*" L. says, with regard to γένηται (the which I have rendered "*may prove,*" though it may only stand for "*may be*"), that it exhibits the 'historic manifestation' as contrasted with the 'absolute being'—the latter finding expression in the ἔστιν of *v.* 17. It seems to me there is in the word the same sense it often bears in Plato and other Greek thinkers. Γίγνεσθαι often means 'to come to be' logically, as the issue of a process of reasoning: in such cases we may render 'is found to be,' or the like. Accordingly, to me, the ἵνα γένηται presents to the mind the irresistible inference that follows the resurrection. The Son is 'first' in Being: He is 'prior' to all Creation, and so high above all things that are—'first' in time (if we may speak of Him in such a connexion, which, strictly speaking, we may not); 'first' in dignity, 'first' every way. This 'first'-ness follows Him in relation to the New Order. There also is He 'first'; first historically (amongst other things);

for was it not He that first 'rose from the dead'? Ἐν πᾶσιν does not mean so much 'in all things' as 'everywhere.' It is an adverbial phrase with 'local' signification. Αὐτός bears a common idiomatic force. 'We are ourselves' is a regular Greek way of saying 'We are alone,' 'We are by ourselves.' Therefore I render "*in Himself.*" The term simply emphasises the Son's unique position. Πρωτεύων (*principatum tenens,* Vulg.) is found only here in N.T. As part of a compound verb we have it in 3 St. John, ὁ φιλοπρωτεύων αὐτῶν Διοτρεφής ("*Diotrophes, who loveth to have the pre-eminence among them*"). The "*pre-eminence*" of our traditional English is fine, but it rather calls for a sacrifice of other words in the sentence. "*That in all things He might have the pre-eminence*" is in truth hardly enough to represent the original. It had been better to have employed the term 'pre-eminent.'

So far we have predicated, or have heard the Apostle predicate, tremendous things of the Son. But more, infinitely more, remains. On we are swept irresistibly to the awe-inspiring pronouncement of *v.* 19. The Lord Christ is 'first' everywhere for no other reason than this, that He is GOD, *completely* GOD. This all-important truth is set forth in the following words:

i. 19. ". . . For in Him was He pleased there should dwell all the Plenitude (of the Godhead) † bodily †."

"*Was He pleased.*" *Whose* 'good pleasure' is

this that is here presented? Is it the Father's? Is it the Son's? Or are we to adopt the remaining alternative and regard πᾶν τὸ πλήρωμα ("*all the plenitude*") as the subject? The context, I think, decides, and carries conviction with it. Grammatically either the second or the third alternative would do admirably *for v.* 19. *Neither* will serve for the following verse. "*He was pleased*" *must refer* to the Father, because "*and by His means to reconcile all things . . .*" can hardly be understood in any other way. Contemplate for a moment this version!

". . . Because He (The Son) was pleased that in Him (*i.e.* in Himself) should have its dwelling the totality of the Deity; and by Him" (that is, by Himself: the language of *v.* 20 will allow no other interpretation. We cannot say "*thereby,*" that is, 'by means of the Plenitude': good grammar it would be, but no sense at all!) "to reconcile all things unto Himself."

Consideration will show that there is no relation at all between the two things stated. The mind wholly fails to trace any logical connexion. But there is all the connexion in the world between the 'perfect Godhead' of *the Son*—the Incarnate Son, that is, unless I err: I will explain why I think so, directly—and *His* effectual Agency in Reconciliation or Atonement. "*Call Christ then the illimitable God!*"

A like logical difficulty eliminates the other alternative. The section is 'broken-backed' and virtually robbed of all meaning if we adopt such a version as this:

"for in Him all the Plenitude was pleased to dwell, and by Him to reconcile the whole of things. . . ."

It ought to conclude "*to Itself.*" But it ends εἰς αὐτόν ("*to Himself*"). Moreover (as L. argues) such a personification of "Pleroma" is definitely late Gnostic: it cannot be Pauline.

Once again, it remains that we should render like this:

"For in Him the Eternal Father was pleased that all the plenitude (of the Deity) should dwell" (or, better, "take up its dwelling") "and (so) by His means to reconcile all things that are to Himself."

Surely the statement so phrased is altogether satisfying. Scripturally the 'reconciliation' of fallen man to God is always represented as the Eternal Father's Will. It is His, the Father's, Love that lies behind it all. Moreover, the verb εὐδοκεῖν (as a term applied to God) invariably refers to the First Person of the Trinity. Old Testament association maybe had influence in deciding it should be so. Anyhow, so it is. Before I say a word about the term πλήρωμα ('plenitude') I should like to clear out of the way the infinitive κατοικῆσαι. This ought to mean (in 'scientific' Greek; I mean Greek of the strictest 'Greekness') "*should take up its dwelling.*" Does it here? Ah! who shall tell? There would seem to be (I speak with every possible hesitation) a certain propriety in regarding this 'good pleasure' of the Father as related *not* to the Son, in His Eternal Being, but in regard of His Incarnation. A good many people nowadays have disposed of all idea of 'atonement' *by sacrifice.* But any effective atonement, extending to all mankind, is only conceivable if Christ be God—if St. John spoke truth when he said, "*The Word became flesh.*" I find it very hard to refer the declaration "*was pleased that in Him all the Plenitude should dwell*" to the Son, regarded as *the Eternal Son.* But that His 'Godhead' (so to speak) should go with Him to Earth, that is a wholly different idea, and a fruitful, indeed an essential one. And now one word about the obelised "*bodily*" of my paraphrase.

Modern editors do not read the adverb σωματικῶς. I cannot help fancying it should stand. There are excellent reasons why it should not be read (altogether apart from textual evidence). The word is liable to misunderstanding. *It has nothing whatever to do with the thought of Incarnation.* It means 'bodily,' as we use 'bodily' in ordinary speech. That is, it is merely equivalent to 'entirely,' 'altogether.' "*Substantially*" might be a fair rendering in this place. We shall come to the word again when we consider chapter ii. 9. Meanwhile I will only say that I should like to keep it here. If it must go, it must. We can manage without it. I do not believe it refers, either here or in chapter ii., *in itself,* to the Incarnation.

Before leaving *v.* 19, we must deal with πλήρωμα. The word is obviously a verbal noun of a very common type. L. lays it down in his famous note that such words are essentially passive. Later scholarship has wisely decided that it would be safer to class them as 'concrete.' It must be admitted that L. was driven to very sad shifts to make good his position. *Κάλυμμα* (which means a 'covering') he declared draws its sense from a bye-meaning of the verb from which it is derived, *i.e.* to 'wrap round.' Thereby he was enabled to preserve the 'passive' sense he postulated. Yet 'covering' is palpably right, and the word is only a concrete noun which comes from the verb to 'cover.' *Πλήρωμα* similarly means a 'filling' or 'fulfilling.' The sense varies in accordance with the varying senses of the parent verb, 'fill,' 'fulfil,' 'complete' (and so forth). This (it would seem, the orthodox doctrine as to nouns in *-μα*) I first found in Sanday and Headlam's *Romans.* In N.T. the word *πλήρωμα* is not by any means a common one. In the Synoptic Gospels it occurs but thrice: in a Marco-Matthean parallel, *αἴρει τὸ πλήρωμα ἀπ' αὐτοῦ* (St. Mark ii. 21), rendered rather dubiously, in R.V., "*that which should fill it up, taketh from it*" (speaking of the incongruously patched garment); and in the curious phrase *σφυρίδων πληρώματα κλασμάτων* ("*basketsful of broken pieces*"). The Fourth Gospel has it used definitely for "*fulness*": "*for of His fulness have we all received*" (*ὅτι ἐκ τοῦ πληρώματος αὐτοῦ ἡμεῖς πάντες ἐλάβομεν*). In Romans we have it four times; twice in xi., once in xiii., and once in xv. The last ("*with fulness of blessing*") is not unlike the Johannine use. In 1 Corinthians we have it once, in an O.T. phrase ("*the earth is the Lord's and the fulness of it*"). In Galatians it occurs in a temporal phrase ("*the fulness of time*"). In Ephesians we have it four times: used temporally in i. 10; again in i. 23 (as quoted above); in iii. 19, in the phrase "*that ye may be fulfilled unto all the fulness of God*" (ἵνα πληρωθῆτε εἰς πᾶν τὸ πλήρωμα τοῦ Θεοῦ), speaking of that Divinely planned perfection to which Christians shall attain; and lastly, in iv. 13, in a somewhat parallel phrase, "*till we all shall come . . . unto a perfect Man, unto the measure of the stature of the perfection of the Christ*" (μέχρι καταντήσωμεν οἱ πάντες εἰς ἄνδρα τέλειον, εἰς μέτρον ἡλικίας τοῦ πληρώματος τοῦ Χριστοῦ). In Colossians it comes twice, both times in the same sense in an almost identical phrase. This phrase stands quite alone, as compared with any other in N.T. It is definitely used in a sense which *may be* technical; which L. considers *is* technical. 'To both alike,' he says (speaking of the Apostle and the Colossians), 'it conveyed the same idea, the totality of the divine powers, or attributes, or agencies, or manifestations.' Apparently also the word is found employed by early heretics (as it most certainly was by later) in a sense very closely akin. Some Gnostics taught that 'the Christ' having descended on Jesus at his baptism *iterum revolasse in suum pleroma* ('once more returned in His own *pleroma*'; see L., p. 264, edition of 1876, in note on πλήρωμα). Cerinthus may have taught so, but of this there is no certitude.

On the other hand, it is plain that the phrase may be St. Paul's own. It obviously is well fitted to express what he wished to assert, viz. the 'full

Godhead' of Our Lord. To be sure, there is one fact which tells against this view with considerable force. That is the elliptical character of the expression, as we have it. Here we read simply "*all the plenitude*," used precisely as if the phrase carried its own interpretation; which it palpably does not. In the other place of occurrence we have it fully expanded in a way that would preclude any possible mistake as to the Apostolic meaning. In ii. 9 the "*plenitude*" (which is said to "*dwell*" in Him "*bodily*") is expressly characterised as "*the plenitude of the Godhead*" (τὸ πλήρωμα τῆς θεότητος). Were it here as there, no need would arise at all for supposing that *pleroma* was already a familiar term to the ears and minds of Colossians. Anyhow, "*all the fulness*" inevitably must mean "*all the fulness of the Godhead*." By itself the expression might cover no more than 'all that makes God God.' The doctrinal statement before us requires no more than this. All that is needed for the immediate purpose is that Christ should be "*perfect God*." Any *esoteric* signification, which the word may have borne, either afterwards or already when St. Paul was writing, is really beside the mark. A strong reason for supposing that the later Gnostic sense is not in the word is just *that it is not wanted.* We can understand the passage entirely well without it. Moreover, the actual phrase (of course, in its fuller form; that one must admit) is precisely such a phrase as the writer might have coined.

i. 20. ". . . and through Him to reconcile 'all things' unto Himself, having made peace through the blood of His cross—by Him (I say) whether things on earth or things in the heavens."

In this verse any English rendering must of necessity cast a veil over one great difficulty. "*Having made peace*," one would say, must refer to our one great Peacemaker—that is, to Christ Himself. But (unless the case is 'irrational,' which, of course, is not inconceivable) the participle *εἰρηνοποιήσας* ("*having made peace*") must refer to the subject of *εὐδόκησεν*; and that, we have decided, refers to the Father Himself. The 'reconciling' of 'all things to Himself' we had better understand as meaning no less than this—the words call for some expansion—"reconciling everything *to* Himself *and bringing everything to Him.* The *εἰς αὐτόν*, I mean, is 'pregnant.' One does not *ἀποκαταλλάσσειν εἰς*: the proper construction is with the dative (as in Ephes. ii. 16). The *εἰς αὐτόν* shadows forth the idea of God, as "*All in all*" (1 Cor. xv.), which we have referred to already. Τὰ *πάντα* ("*all things*") is a term of the widest possible connotation. The context alone can narrow it. Here perhaps it can hardly cover 'inanimate' things (yet see Romans, chapter viii.), but it certainly covers things 'animate,' such as are not of our world. The *διὰ τοῦ αἵματος τοῦ σταυροῦ αὐτοῦ* is a phrase more fully defining the *δι' αὐτοῦ* which precedes it. It is not enough to say "*through Him to reconcile* . . .": the writer must needs add "*by means of the blood of His Cross*." Mark then that the death of Christ (can "*the blood of His Cross*" mean aught else?) is for

St. Paul of the first importance. Εἰρηνοποιήσας ("*having peace made*"), one is not surprised to find, is here only in N.T., though once it occurs in LXX.

The Apostle has now vindicated the unique position and dignity of his Master and only Saviour as against all wild ideas which might be abroad in Colossæ. He is God, altogether God; and as such all-powerful to achieve the mighty ends which the Father has in view. By His means and agency 'all things' can be reconciled. Passing on, he applies the teaching to the people he is addressing:

i. 21. "Aye, and you that once were estranged and enemies in disposition, while you worked your evil works . . ."

Up to this point all is plain. We need only to remark that the participle "*estranged*" (ἀπηλλοτριωμένους) bears witness to a 'fall.' It was not always so with man. Further, that διανοίᾳ implies mental attitude. Lastly, that ἐν τοῖς ἔργοις τοῖς πονηροῖς ('*in your evil deeds*') is most satisfactorily taken as a 'temporal' expression. Now the difficulties begin; difficulties of reading first, and then difficulties of attachment to what has gone before. There are three readings to choose from. None of them connects itself quite regularly with the context. But that we hardly expect. St. Paul is as Thucydides: his grammar is all his own. He is bound by no conventions of the Schoolroom. The readings are as follows:

(1) ἀποκατηλλάγητε (the Vatican MS. only).

(2) ἀποκαταλλαγέντες (a 'Western' reading, classed

by L. as 'correction,' and faulty correction at that. It is not in the case we want: it ought to be accusative).

(3) ἀποκατήλλαξεν (the ordinary reading of most MSS.).

Observe how all of these involve certain difficulties. Ἀποκατήλλαξεν ("*He hath reconciled*") agrees admirably with the statement in the verse that is next above. There we read, "*He* (the Father) *was pleased to reconcile all things to Himself by means of Him* (the Son)." So the finite verb "*He has reconciled*" would seem simply to pick up and repeat what there was said. It is a small thing (and wholly 'Pauline') that we should have a finite active verb thus coupled irregularly with a passive participle. We are then left with, "*You once being estranged . . . but now hath He reconciled*"—a sentence obviously irregular in regard to its composition. That, however, need not surprise us. The really substantial objection to the reading ἀποκατήλλαξεν lies in this: it is wholly out of harmony with what follows. Ἀποκατήλλαξεν in this sentence (as it stands) can only refer to the Son, because the words go on, "*by His incarnate Body, by means of death.*" It will be seen that *vv.* 19 and 21 are very puzzling indeed in regard of their subject: I mean the question, Who is the 'He' contained in their leading verbs, εὐδόκησεν in the one case, ἀποκατήλλαξεν (if we read it) in the other? It follows that, if we decide to read ἀποκατήλλαξεν, we must place a full stop at the end of *v.* 20, and make a fresh start altogether. The word παραστῆσαι ("*present*"), to which we shall come anon, is not altogether without influence in deciding the weighty question.

W. H. (it should be noticed) retain this particular reading, but they treat it as a parenthesis, apparently meaning to render "*however now He hath reconciled you* . . .": it is only putting off the trouble, so far as I can see. The difficulty of connexion still remains. R.V. also has kept this reading. L. boldly follows B. (the Vatican MS.). He regards the Eternal Father as being still the subject (that is, in the writer's mind; for we have no definite verb to match the subject) and carries on *εὐδόκησεν* ("*He was pleased*") from *v.* 19 above. This requires us to disregard the palpable difficulty involved in the phrase "*in the Body of His flesh,*" where we should require (if we could have it) "by the Body of the flesh *of His Son.*"

However, L.'s reading would render (as I suppose),

"Moreover you that once were estranged and enemies in disposition (in the days when your works were evil)"—this phrase, though differently rendered, as before—". . . but now you have been reconciled by the Body of His incarnation"—the readers must see for themselves that this 'His' refers to the Son: it can have no other reference—". . . (He hath been pleased) to present you . . ."

which gives us (as it happens) a supererogatory "*you*" (*ὑμᾶς*), which we would sooner be without.

There are puzzles every way. Yet the actual doctrinal statement is plain as plain can be. It is simply, you *were* estranged; *now* you are estranged no more; you have been *reconciled*: this reconciliation comes through Christ's death; and you shall be 'presented' all blameless before God's sight. Accordingly, here (as elsewhere) the 'plain man' need not vex his soul over verbal difficulties. The meaning clearly shines forth from all the mists of language, though the language, it must be admitted, is often abundantly misty.

L., by the way, detects a special suitability in the passive ἀποκαταλλάγητε (comparing Rom. v. 10). But the ἀποκαταλλάξαι above proves that the active is to the full as suitable as the passive. That it is 'the mind of man, not the mind of God, which must undergo a change' is doubtless true enough.

On the whole, I think, I should side with W. H. and the Revisers and keep the familiar reading. This has, at least, one great advantage: it makes the second "*you*" no longer supererogatory. The one little word we have too many in this case is the δέ that follows νυνί. We must treat it precisely as if it did not exist, and, placing a full stop at the end of *v.* 20, pass on with a change of subject.

Two phrases in *v.* 22 call for some consideration. One is "*the Body of His flesh*." This plainly can only mean 'the Body of His incarnation' (the only 'body' wherein He could die), as opposed to His mystical 'Body' mentioned only four verses back. L. compares a phrase from Ecclesiasticus, ἄνθρωπος πόρνος ἐν σώματι σαρκὸς αὐτοῦ, which is, however (I suppose), a Hebraic pleonasm; whereas here the σαρκός is demanded by the claims of explicitness.

The other is the word "*present*" (παραστῆσαι). In St. Luke ii. 22 precisely the same word is used of the 'presentation' in the Temple. In Acts i. 3 it is found in the curious expression παρέστησεν ἑαυτὸν ζῶντα ("He *shewed* Himself alive"), where to the idea of presentation is added that of demonstration. The sense of demonstration, pure and simple, is found in Acts xxiv. 13. At first sight the sense in our passage would seem to be the 'presentation' sense, the idea of solemn presentation before the Throne of God. Such a 'presentation' of a man by himself we have three or four times in Romans. But this is not exactly that. In 1 Corinthians it is found in the unusual sense 'commend,' a sense it could hardly bear, were it not for the context. "Meat will not *commend* you to God" is the statement in viii. 8. In 2 Corinthians there are two instances, each of them of interest. In xi. 2 we find the Apostle using these words of himself: "for I am jealous over you with a godly jealousy; for I espoused you to one husband (ἡρμοσάμην ἑνὶ ἀνδρί), that I might *present* you" (literally, 'for to present you,' the infinitive just as here) "as a pure virgin to the Christ." The other is yet more striking and rather unexpected. It is in chapter iv. 14. It runs as follows:

"being sure that He Who raised the Lord Jesus will raise us too with Jesus and will 'present' us with you" (παραστήσει σὺν ὑμῖν).

I call the wording unexpected because, apparently,

it attributes the act of 'presentation' to the God who raises; whereas one would suppose that Our Lord, as the Redeemer, would 'present' His redeemed to God. L. thinks that in our passage too it is God Himself who 'presents.' This involves a 'presentation' of what one would be inclined to style a 'one-sided' character. We feel (and can hardly help feeling) that the whole conception requires a second and different person to be presented to. Much the same question raises itself in connexion with Ephes. v. 25-27. This difficult passage says:

"As Christ loved the Church and gave Himself up for it, that He might sanctify it, purifying it with the washing (λουτρῷ) of water with the word, that he might † 'present' to Himself † His Church a glorious Church" (*ἵνα παραστήσῃ αὐτὸς ἑαυτῷ ἔνδοξον τὴν ἐκκλησίαν*).

The *αὐτὸς ἑαυτῷ* here is undeniably puzzling. It may well represent the advantage or profit of the subject; that is, it may mean '*for* Himself' rather than '*to* Himself.' The Vulgate says *ut exhiberet ipse sibi,* where I take it the verb must stand for something else than 'presenting.' There remain yet two further places where the verb bears a secondary sense, a sense other than 'set' or 'place beside,' its original signification. One comes in *v.* 28 of the chapter before us, "*that I may manage to 'present' every man perfect in Christ*"; the other is in 2 Timothy ii. 15, "*Give diligence to 'present' thyself approved unto God*" (*σεαυτὸν δόκιμον παραστῆσαι τῷ Θεῷ*).

As one ponders on all these passages it is borne in on the mind that, while 'present' is a suitable meaning in such places as contain a dative of the person to whom 'presentation' is made, some other rendering had better be found for places where such a dative is not easily supplied nor (if there at all) intelligible.

In such a passage as ours '*display*' would seem to be the sort of sense demanded. It is really not much more than 'make'; though 'make in the presence of witnesses' would be a more accurate rendering. In Ephes. v. (*l.c.*) I would suggest "*that He might 'make' for Himself His Church a 'palpably' glorious Church*"; the 'palpably' and the 'make' together contributing to make up the full force of the *παραστήσῃ*, while the *αὐτὸς ἑαυτῷ* would set before us the supreme satisfaction (if we may say so) of Him who achieves this supreme end. Similarly here I would like to paraphrase:

i. 22. (conclusion of verse). ". . . to display you holy and blameless before Him and beyond the reach of any charge . . ."

The *κατενώπιον αὐτοῦ* (the curious compound *κατενώπιον* has been found, used of the Divine Presence, in a Christian papyrus — no doubt influenced by Pauline language) must be taken as independent of the *παραστῆσαι*, adding a further idea to those contained in the adjectives; not only 'holy' but '*holy in His Presence.*' Ephes. i. 4 presents an exact parallel. Ἁγίους of necessity bears an ethical force. Ἀμώμους may mean 'unblemished,' as L. argues, but that figurative sense (for the term would be a ritual one) seems rather out of place considering its position in the triad. Ἀνεγκλήτους literally means 'unimpeachable,' 'unexceptionable.'

This blessed consummation can only be attained provided they maintain faith unimpaired. To lose that is to lose all. Therefore the proviso follows:

i. 23. ". . . Provided that" (εἴ γε, in Vulgate curiously '*si tamen*') "ye stay on in Faith, firm founded and stedfast, and not inclined to move from the hope of the Gospel which ye heard, which has been proclaimed in every corner of the creation under heaven, whereof I Paul have been an instrument."

Ἐπιμένειν is employed, as three times in Romans (vi. 1 and xi. 22, 23), each time with a dative of the thing (τῇ ἁμαρτίᾳ, τῇ χρηστότητι, τῇ ἀπιστίᾳ) in which one 'stays on.' As 'sin' and 'unbelief' have the definite article there, so 'faith' has it here. We need not concern ourselves to translate the article. It is simply 'faith'; neither 'the faith' nor 'your faith.' Τεθεμελιωμένοι and ἑδραῖοι (I think) go closely together: μὴ μετακινούμενοι expresses a result of the foregoing 'stedfastness.' I have said "*inclined to move,*" rather than "*moved,*" because the Greek tense states no more than that. As for 'the hope,' it belongs to 'the Gospel' or comes from the Gospel. Ἐν πάσῃ κτίσει is an expression closely parallel to ἐν παντὶ τῷ κόσμῳ, which we had in *v.* 6 above. It does not mean that the Gospel has pervaded the world completely, only that it has made its way into every quarter. Τῇ ὑπὲρ τὸν οὐρανόν is added because the writer would limit the 'creation' indicated. He speaks of the world of men. In the appendix of St. Mark we have κηρύξατε τὸ εὐαγγέλιον πάσῃ τῇ κτίσει ('Proclaim the Gospel to all the creation'). What the relation of that may be to the language of St. Paul it is not easy to decide.

"*Of which I Paul have been an instrument.*" He does not mean to imply that his glorious labours are over. It is merely that he is overwhelmed with the sense of God's wonderful goodness in employing him in His work. I say 'instrument,' rather than 'agent,' because it is the figure we usually employ in such a context. 'Agent' is just a commercial term, which 'instrument' is not. The sense of either is right to express the original.

The paragraph that follows starts in a very unusual way. "*Now I rejoice,*" it says. The English reader will say, Oh, but 'nows' are common enough at the opening of a new section! And that is very true. But those are not this sort of 'now.' In 1 Cor. xv. we have "But *now* is Christ risen from the dead" (νυνὶ δὲ Χριστὸς ἐγήγερται); yet even that is not quite precisely the same as this.

Somehow the thought of his own high privilege and the thought of their great hope seem so to have worked on his feelings that he breaks out into jubilant thanksgiving. It would appear he does not always feel in a thankful mood. But now he does.

i. 24. ". . . Oh, now I rejoice in my sufferings for your sakes and so far as in me lies fill up in my poor person what is lacking in Christ's afflictions for His Body's sake, which is the Church. . . ."

In this verse there are verbal difficulties: there are also difficulties of dogma. For what the Apostle is saying it is not quite easy to see, and yet it is very important we should make no error about it. The verbal difficulty centres in the two phrases with ὑπέρ. The ὑπὲρ ὑμῶν ("*on your behalf*") might attach itself to the words "*I rejoice,*" but it almost certainly does not. It is far more likely to be "*my sufferings on your behalf*" (what I have to bear for your sakes). And yet, we ask ourselves, in what sense can St. Paul be said to bear anything for them at all? He has never preached to them: his present imprisonment, with all its privations, is in no way due to them, nor has anything to do with them. How then is he suffering *on their behalf?* The other ὑπέρ and its noun are also puzzling. Once again, there plainly lies before us a choice of interpretations. It may be the "*afflictions of Christ on behalf of His Body*" are set in contrast with "*my sufferings for you.*" Against this is to be set the insertion of the words "*in my flesh*" (ἐν τῇ σαρκί μου) between the name Christ and the phrase in dispute. Or, again, it is very possible that the words "*in behalf of His Body*" pick up and as it were define with a larger accuracy the "*on your behalf*" that precedes them.

On the whole this latter alternative commends itself as the likelier. Παθήματα perhaps implies a lesser degree of pain to be borne than does the following θλίψεις. In itself a πάθημα may be a very trivial thing: a θλίψις hardly can.

The very difficult clause ἀνταναπληρῶ τὰ ὑστερήματα τῶν θλίψεων τοῦ Χριστοῦ ("I fill up what is lacking in Christ's afflictions") calls for much consideration. The "*afflictions of Christ*" may obviously express three separate things:

Either (1) the afflictions that Christ actually bore in achieving our redemption.

Or (2) the afflictions which belong not to the Incarnate Christ but to Christ in so far as He may be identified with His Church.

Or (3) such afflictions as at all time belong to God's 'Anointed.' In this case the phrase would correspond to the "*reproach of the Christ*" (τὸν ὀνειδισμὸν τοῦ Χριστοῦ) to which reference is made in Hebrews xi. 26.

A combination of (1) and (2) would seem to be best and wisest. We feel certain the Apostle did not mean to imply that Christ's Death and Passion had anything 'lacking' in it. That was altogether complete to achieve His purpose. But the sufferings Christ suffered in His own Person on Earth and the sufferings He suffers mystically in the sufferings of His saints are apparently regarded by the writer as all one—united together in some manner which it is not altogether easy for us to comprehend.

The expression ἀνταναπληρῶ τὰ ὑστερήματα (as L. carefully points out) means "*I, for my part, fill up, supplement, the points that are lacking. . .*"

The genitive, in our Version rendered "*of the sufferings of Christ*," is more properly represented by "*in.*" The case expresses the sum total, in which there may be 'deficiency' (ὑστέρημα is a piece of 'shortage') at one point or another. In 2 Cor. i. 5, we have, "*as the sufferings of Christ overflow unto us*" (καθὼς περισσεύει τὰ παθήματα τοῦ Χριστοῦ εἰς ἡμᾶς), but that is not nearly so bold a statement of the case and has nothing to perplex the reader. Speaking broadly, it is not so much the conception of "*filling up the sufferings of Christ*" (for that, in a mystical sense, one can easily understand) which causes our perplexity, as the ὑπὲρ ὑμῶν and the ὑπὲρ τοῦ σώματος. There lies the *crux* of the matter, as I think. Probably all we can say about it is simply this: that whatever the believer 'suffers,' in patient faith, because he is Christ's, may somehow be regarded as contributing to the welfare of the Church. It is 'the Mystery of Pain' in the spiritual sphere.

The explanation of Augustine, quoted with approval by L. ('has very much to recommend it'), viz. 'Christ still suffers affliction, not in His own "flesh," for that is ascended, but in the flesh of His servant ("*in my flesh*"),' is invalidated somewhat by the consideration that it tends to empty of meaning the impressive verb ἀνταναπληρῶ. The 'sufferings' in question are really and truly Paul's. It is he who has to bear them; it is he who 'rejoices' in them. No doubt they are entailed by his mystical union with Christ, as a 'member' of His Body. Yet still they remain his only, and here he represents himself as actually 'rejoicing' in them, because he recognises that somehow they are a contribution to the total of Christ's 'afflictions,' and further will have their fruit in blessing for the Church. It is the fact that they are borne 'in Him' and 'for Him' which makes their fruitfulness certain, and justifies (shall we say ?) the double *ὑπέρ*. The Apostolic prison was far enough away, but the distant Church at Colossæ, nay, all the Body of Christ, was somehow affected for good by the patience of the prisoner.

The next few verses to the end of the chapter are a good deal simpler, and may be taken all together.

i. 25-29. ". . . Wherein I became an instrument in accordance with the heavenly 'stewardship' which was committed to me, to reach as far as you, that I should preach God's 'Word' completely—the 'wonderful truth' that was hidden away from ages and generations, but now has been plainly shown to His saints; to whom God has been pleased to make known the grandeur and the glory of this revelation amongst the nations, that is, Christ in you, the great Hope of Glory! Whom we proclaim abroad, warning every man and instructing every man in every 'wisdom,' that we may display (or 'produce') every man fully initiate 'in Christ.' To which end I also toil and strive in accordance with the power that worketh in me mightily."

"*Whereof I was made a minister*," runs our English. I paraphrase it otherwise (not wishing in the least to alter the familiar words in our greatly treasured translation), because the word 'minister' hardly represents διάκονος, which means properly 'agent' or 'instrument'; and, moreover, the genitive ἧς represents a different relation (at least, I incline to think so) from that set forth in the οὗ of *v.* 23. Rightly and truly διάκονος is the 'agent' of a person. One can be 'agent' of the Gospel, but hardly (I think) 'agent' of the Church. One is rather an 'instrument' in bringing about, or building up, the Church. Therefore I say 'Where*in*.' A '*Minister*' of the Church is a wholly different thing. That is altogether intelligible, but it is not what the Apostle has in view.

The conception of 'stewardship' (a common one in St. Paul; cf. 1 Cor. iv. 1, 1 Cor. ix. 17, Ephes. iii. 2) comes directly from Our Lord. He it is Who described His workers by the figure of 'stewardship'; a 'steward' being a higher slave whose function it was to supply the needs of his fellow-servants. It is in St. Luke xii. 42 we find Christ's consecration of a figure which for us, living under wholly different conditions, has lost some part of its force. A care, or charge for others, under the strictest responsibility, is the fundamental idea of it. A "*stewardship of God*" is a stewardship in God's Household conferred by Him on His servant. The expression in 1 Corinthians (iv. 1) will occur to every reader, "So let a man account of us as of underlings of Christ and *stewards of the mysteries of God*" (ὡς ὑπηρέτας Χριστοῦ καὶ οἰκονόμους μυστηρίων Θεοῦ), from which we gather that His 'stewards' have it as their charge to feed His household with *μυστήρια*, presumably the truths of Christian Revelation. Whether the word has special reference to Sacraments (which it must include) is matter of discussion. But it is reasonable to understand it in the broadest possible sense. The *εἰς ὑμᾶς*, grammatically a singular addition, is aptly illustrated by the parallel from Ephesians (iii. 2), "*the 'dispensation'* (in the Latin sense) *of the 'special favour' of God that was given me to you ward*" (*τῆς χάριτος τοῦ Θεοῦ τῆς δοθείσης μοι εἰς ὑμᾶς*). It is possible that "*for you,*" both here and there, would best express the sense of the prepositional phrase. Observe that in Ephesians it is the *χάρις* (the grace) which is given, not the *οἰκονομία* as one would have expected. This makes it plain that *χάρις* must stand for the undeserved privilege conferred on the Apostle. *Οἰκονομία* in that place should possibly be 'administration.' In a Greek papyrus document (No. 28 in Professor George Milligan's delightful little book) we have the words *ἵνα . . . τὴν συνήθη οἰκονομίαν τῆς ἀπογραφῆς πληρώσωσιν*, 'that they may carry out the census after the usual way.' This illustrates at once the derivative sense of *οἰκονομία* ('administration,' 'management') and also the use of *πληροῦν*, which is the next point we have to note. "*To fulfil the word of God*" means 'to preach the Gospel fully' (for that is the usual meaning of the expression "*the word of God*"), both in regard to geographical extent and possibly also fulness of teaching. There is a parallel phrase in Rom. xv. 19.

". . . So that from Jerusalem and all about as far as Illyricum I have fully preached the Gospel of Christ" (πεπληρωκέναι με τὸ εὐαγγέλιον τοῦ Χριστοῦ).

There the Apostle plainly means that he has preached the Gospel everywhere, in all that extensive region. This 'divine message' is characterised as a *μυστήριον*, a great religious truth, and a truth withal concealed. The term is derived, of course, from the well-known 'mysteries' of the ancient world, wherein certain 'esoteric' truths were taught to the initiate. Roughly speaking, the word means 'secret.' The fact that God's revelation in Jesus Christ has been so long time 'hid' constitutes it a 'mystery.' Even now it is confined to the Christian 'initiate,' though indeed there is no reason why any one should not attain to Christian initiation. 'Ages' and 'generations' are terms describing successive periods in the history of humanity. Several 'generations' go to make up one 'age.' In Ephes. iii. 21 we have the remarkable phrase *εἰς πάσας τὰς γενεὰς τοῦ αἰῶνος τῶν αἰώνων*, "*unto all the generations that make up the* (great) *age of the ages*"—a comprehensive expression for "*to all eternity.*" Here, when it is said that the great revelation of the Gospel has been hidden away 'from ages and generations,' it means it has been hidden away from mankind during countless years. I don't think the *ἀπό* is 'temporal.' The 'ages' would seem to stand for the people living in them. But it matters little truly whether it means '*from* many centuries' or '*through* many centuries.' It is 'hidden away' no more. It has been revealed τοῖς ἁγιοῖς αὐτοῦ, "*to His saints.*" The full and dazzling splendour of the gracious purpose of God, concealed from man so long, has now been made fully known. "*The wealth of the glory*" is a regular Pauline combination. He is specially fond of 'wealth' as a figurative term. To the Apostle, speaking as a Jew, the splendour of the Gospel culminated just in this, that it embraced the Gentiles too. Hence the addition of ἐν τοῖς ἔθνεσιν ("amongst the Gentiles"). That God should so wonderfully extend His Mercy was to a Jew an amazing thing. The exact force of ἐν τοῖς ἔθνεσιν is somewhat hard to be sure of. Perhaps we might say that it belongs to τί τὸ πλοῦτος τῆς δόξης. God has been pleased to make known (as it were) the astounding fruitfulness of the Gospel amongst the Gentiles. Or, again, it may be a 'corrective' phrase of a kind, explanatory of οἷς. But we should then have expected it to be introduced by καί, "*yes, even among the Gentiles.*" Plainly the Gentiles are predominant at this moment in the Apostle's thought. The Gospel was marvellous, especially in this, that (in the words of Bishop Lightfoot) 'it overflowed all barriers of caste and sex.' There was nothing 'exclusive' about it. It was open to every one. The best commentary on all the verse is to be found in the opening passage of Ephes. iii. There we find that the mystery of mysteries lies herein—in the idea that the "*Gentiles* are '*fellow-heirs,*' '*fellow-members of the body*' (if that be right), '*fellow-partakers of the promise in Christ Jesus'"* (συγκληρονόμα καὶ σύνσωμα καὶ συνμέτοχα τῆς ἐπαγγελίας). Here the 'mystery' (or 'secret revealed') is defined as "*Christ in you*" (cf. Rom. viii. 10), "Christ in *you*," observe, not "Christ in *us*." I think we must regard it as meaning "*Christ in the Gentiles*." If it be so, our μυστήριον is as the μυστήριον of Ephesians. The "*in*" represents, of course, the thought of Christ 'indwelling.' He is the 'hope of glory' (cf. Rom. viii. 11). This Christ, this 'indwelling' Christ, the Apostle everywhere proclaims: all true Christian preachers proclaim Him. The proclamation (as L. points out) involves two elements; an element of 'warning' (νουθετοῦντες), for 'repentance' is a condition; and an element of 'instruction' (διδάσκοντες). These medicinal processes the Christian preacher applies to all. He does not pick and choose as they do in heathen mysteries. Neither birth, nor wealth, nor learning have any privilege. It is 'every man,' 'every man,' 'every man' (that is, every human being, man, woman, or child), three times over! Nor is *anything* kept from any who would learn. The teaching is "*in all wisdom*" (ἐν πάσῃ σοφίᾳ). The truth is, in these Christian 'Mysteries' (if we may employ the familiar term) every one may be an *epopt* (ἐπόπτης); every one may attain (as it were) to the highest degree. Τέλειος ("*perfect*," *i.e.* fully initiate) was a term in regular use in heathen 'mysteries.' It is St. Paul's interest to bring every man he may to this happy consummation, to make him "*perfect in Christ*." The ἐν Χριστῷ (I think) is added to make the clear even clearer. 'Perfect' he will have them all, "*fully initiate in Christ.*" The τέλειος of 1 Cor. ii. 6 probably is not used in this sense, but means "*full-grown.*" So the American revisers take it. The neighbourhood of 'infants' (νήπιοι) makes that probable. As for ἐν Χριστῷ, it may be interpreted in many ways. Anyhow, a man is τέλειος ἐν Χριστῷ ("perfect in Christ") when he has an adequate grasp, and withal a fruitful grasp, of all fundamental Christian truth. Nothing less than this most complete 'initiation' of every man that will listen (is there any hidden meaning in the singular number of πάντα ἄνθρωπον?) will content the Prince of Missionaries. For this he toils with all his might. And indeed he does not do it of his own strength. There is an ἐνέργεια, a heaven-sent capacity, which works in him; aye, and works ἐν δυνάμει ("with power"). Both δύναμις and ἐνέργεια carry a 'superhuman' sense; the latter invariably. Such an ἐνέργεια can only exist in mortal man if the Spirit of God is with him. Here St. Paul says his ἐνέργεια is actually "*set working in him.*" Ἐνεργουμένην (I feel pretty sure) should be taken as *passive.* Study of the word in a concordance tends to produce this result in the mind.

# CHAPTER II

THE Apostle has now rendered thanks to God for his distant 'Godchildren'—we may call them so, perhaps, because he is not directly their spiritual 'father,'—he has commended the zeal of their Evangelist and the purity of his teaching; he has spoken of his prayers for their growth in spiritual knowledge and in the Christian life. Anon he has discoursed of Christ and His unique position both in regard to all Creation and to the Church. In Him resides the *pleroma*; *in Him*, because It so resides, is the Reconciliation for fallen man, for man 'estranged' from God, the Reconciliation for the Colossians themselves. The Apostle, as he dwells on it all, is filled with a strange joy, that he should have been so privileged as to be permitted to bear a part in the glorious work of proclaiming the new revelation, this mystery of mysteries. It is his one ambition to do it with all his might (God helping him, as He does), and to do it absolutely.

Chapter ii. opens with the expression of his great anxiety for Colossæ and the sister Churches. They have a great deal yet to learn; they have much false teaching to resist. Above all, they must cleave to CHRIST, with a fuller realisation of what He is, and what He is for themselves.

Accordingly the new section begins:

ii. 1-3. "For I would have you know what a struggle I have for you and the people at Laodicea—in fact, for all that have not seen my face in bodily presence; (praying) that their hearts be comforted and that they be knit together in love and (attain) to all the wealth of the fulness of understanding, unto a fuller knowledge of the 'mystery' of God, CHRIST that is, in Whom are all the stores of 'wisdom' and 'knowledge,' † hidden away" †.

The opening formula presents us with the less common 'positive' variety of the more usual negative 'I would not have you ignorant.' The ἀγῶνα of the first verse may pick up the ἀγωνιζόμενος of the last verse of chapter i., but I rather suspect it does not. Therefore I have not troubled to suggest any such connection in the paraphrase. The ἀγών ('struggle') is an ἀγών of prayer, or at least prayer is the outcome of it. Apostolic anxiety invariably finds its vent in that most natural outlet. As L. pertinently observes, one cannot be wholly certain that the Colossians and the Laodiceans are included amongst the "*all, who have not seen my face.*" But the αὐτῶν of *v.* 2 makes it very natural: the "*they*" latent in that "*their*" plainly covers all the communities, the Colossian and Laodicean as well as the others. So ὅσοι οὐχ ἑώρακαν ("*all that have not seen*") had better be regarded as inclusive. We could have wished the Apostle had named more of these Asiatic Christian bodies. No doubt Hierapolis was one of them. The ἵνα παρακληθῶσιν of *v.* 2 ("*that their hearts be comforted*") gives the scope and tenor of his prayer. The participle συμβιβασθέντες is, for all intents and purposes, equivalent to a new clause "*and that they*" (as opposed to their 'hearts') "*be knit together in love.*" This use of the participle, to add a new statement, is not unlike the usage we find in Acts and in Hebrews. See, for instance, Acts xxv. 13, where ἀσπασάμενοι is very properly rendered in R.V. "*and saluted.*" "*Knit together*" is not, perhaps, a very convincing translation. It is not absolutely certain what συμβιβασθέντες implies. Sometimes it means '*instruct*,' sometimes '*conclude*,' '*infer*' (literally, 'putting two and two together'). Here *v.* 19 below and the parallel in Ephesians lead us to suppose that some such idea as 'building up' or 'compacting' is what is required. But the immediate context suggests that it is not a '*corporate*' result the Apostle has in view, but rather an effect to be produced on separate individuals. On the other hand, we may take ἐν ἀγάπῃ ("*in love*") very closely with συμβιβασθέντες and regard that one short phrase as 'corporate' in effect ("*built up together in love*"; cf. iii. 14), assuming what follows next, the growth in 'understanding' and 'knowledge,' to apply to the separate members of the several communities. Love is a social virtue, but 'knowledge' (one would think) belongs to the individual. The phrases "*all the wealth of the fulness of understand-*

*ing*" and "*the fuller knowledge of God's mystery*" are virtually synonymous; the second defines more nearly the vaguer language of the first. Πληροφορία (it should be said) is a rather difficult word. Our R.V. translates it "*assurance*" (which L. affirms to be its regular N.T. meaning), with marginal variant "*fulness.*" 'Assurance' in this place is not the sense we need. The term (I suppose) is really a harvest metaphor. 'Full-bearing' is what it means. Perhaps its real significance is '*rich fulness*,' or the like. Some day, no doubt, ancient documents will help us to its right meaning. The corresponding verb, which is mostly found in the passive voice, means (1) 'fulfil' (2 Tim. iv. 5), or 'be fulfilled' (St. Luke i. 1; 2 Tim. iv. 17), in all which places it seems equivalent to πληροῦν; (2) 'be fully convinced' (thrice in Romans). Πληροφορία of σύνεσις ("fulness of understanding") is obviously much the same thing as ἐπίγνωσις τοῦ μυστηρίου ("larger knowledge of the mystery").

At this point there are variants. The reading of B. is τοῦ Θεοῦ Χριστοῦ: this L. classes as 'original.' W. H. suspect a primitive corruption of a reading τοῦ ἐν Χριστῷ. This is actually read in one 'cursive' manuscript. Τοῦ Θεοῦ is read alone; also τοῦ Χριστοῦ alone; also τοῦ Θεοῦ ὅ ἐστιν Χριστός (an obviously 'interpretative' variant). The *textus receptus* reads τοῦ Θεοῦ καὶ πατρὸς καὶ τοῦ Χριστοῦ. This is rendered in A.V., "*the mystery of God and of the Father and of Christ.*" R.V. (with modern editors) accepts the simplest and shortest reading, "*the mystery of God, even Christ.*" I think it may be said that this meets the general requirements of the situation infinitely best. 'Christ first, Christ last, Christ everywhere' is the Pauline position. Other men teach other 'mysteries,' other momentous religious 'secrets.' For St. Paul all religious 'mystery' (all any man needs to know for his soul's weal) is concentrated in Him. He is emphatically "the mystery *of God*," as contrasted with all others whatsoever emanating from a *human* origin. Let us then be well content to take it so. Θεοῦ Χριστοῦ must not in any case (as L. warns) be taken together. That is against all Pauline usage. For the definition of "*God's mystery*" as 'Christ' L. well compares the celebrated passage in 1 Tim. iii. 16:

> "And confessedly great is the mystery of godliness (τὸ μυστήριον τῆς εὐσεβείας), *Who* was manifested in the flesh (ὃς ἐφανερώθη ἐν σαρκί). . . ."

The ὅς there, as the Χριστοῦ here, very plainly identifies the 'mystery' with Christ Himself.

Of Him it is here said, that He is a very 'storehouse' of all 'wisdom.' It is all contained in Him. The words σοφία and γνῶσις had both of them (at the time St. Paul wrote), and especially the latter, a 'cant' significance. *Gnosis* was a term much affected by those who laid claim to possess an 'esoteric' knowledge. We cannot tell whether here such senses (or such a sense) are in the writer's mind, or whether he merely employs the words as they are in fact employed in the Greek Old Testament. 'Hidden treasures' (θησαυροὶ ἀπόκρυφοι) is a Septuagint expression. But perhaps that has nothing to do with the usage here before us.

The position of ἀπόκρυφοι (R.V., "in Whom are all the treasures of knowledge *hidden*") throws undoubted emphasis on it. This suggests a covert reference to the secret stores of knowledge (γνῶσις) which certain superior persons laid claim to possess. Compare the well-known passage in 1 Timothy (vi. 20), where γνῶσις is oddly rendered 'science' in A.V. Such *gnosis* was passed from hand to hand in secret writings, technically known by the term '*apocryphal.*' This adjective, literally meaning no more than merely 'hidden,' first used by such pretentious teachers as a term of distinction and honour, came by consequence to bear, amongst orthodox believers, the sense 'heretical.' Our use of 'apocryphal' (for writings not included in the Canon of Holy Writ) is entirely modern.

All 'wisdom,' all 'knowledge' (says the writer) is 'hidden away' in Christ. So 'hidden,' it is not hidden; it is open to every one. Once again, our holy religion knows nothing of caste: it has no inner and outer 'circles.' All who profess the contrary are merely heretics. For me, I incline to think that in the full compound phrase, "*all the treasures of wisdom and knowledge hidden away,*" "*treasures of wisdom*" is O.T. in association and derivation, while '*knowledge*' and '*hidden away*' are placed where they are in the sentence because they have a reference to erroneous and false teachings in vogue in the parts of Colossæ. To all such vain imaginings the Apostle opposes Christ. A great deal of ingenuity, both here and in other connexions, has been brought into play by those who would wish to discriminate the two terms 'wisdom' (σοφία) and 'knowledge' (γνῶσις). In some cases the explanations are actually contradictory, the *gnosis* of one scholar being the *sophia* of another!

If I may venture to suggest a new distinction (where maybe no distinction at all is needed), it would be this. Σοφία is a Jewish term; γνῶσις a Gentile and a Greek one. Hellenic 'thought' is opposed to Israelitish 'wisdom.' To argue that one is 'intuitive,' the other 'ratiocinative,' is (I believe) beside the mark. They denote a different standpoint: that is all. The Apostle says, in effect, "Call it what you will! call it σοφία, if you be an adherent of Jewish ideas; or γνῶσις, if you be not uninfluenced by Hellenism: I tell you, *all* of it—all 'knowledge' that is really worth having—is centred wholly in *Christ.*"

He continues:

ii. 4. 5. "I say it for fear any should delude you with specious talk. For although I am away in bodily presence yet in spirit I am with you, rejoicing (in you) and beholding your orderly array, the solid front presented by your faith towards Christ. . . ."

It is a curious thing, but so it is, that such Pauline phrases as "*this I say,*" "*on this account,*" or the like, are often exceedingly difficult to explain with certainty. This particular formula generally refers forwards (see 1 Cor. i. 12, Gal. iii. 17, Ephes. iv. 17, 1 Thess. iv. 15). It generally stands for "*I mean this*," introducing an explanation. Here it cannot: it must refer to what has just been said. Now the statement just made is, that the writer desires them to know how anxious he is about them. To which, characteristically, he appends a mention of the direction which his anxiety takes in prayer. He is anxious for them to come to a larger knowledge of Christ. Indeed, the foregoing sentence ends with a definite dogmatic assertion about Christ (as we have seen).

What then is the reference of the *τοῦτο* ("*this* I say")? Is it the mention of his anxiety? Is it the prayer which that suggests to him? Or is it the statement contained in the clause immediately preceding about Christ Himself? The mention of 'delusion' suggests the last of the three. On the other hand, the rest of the context decidedly suggests that the reference is rather to the Apostolic anxiety—a thing of which they could have no knowledge without his assurance. The thought of his presence 'in spirit' will help them to resist specious suggestions from any quarter—*ἵνα μηδείς*; is there not in the word an insinuation that the contemplated enemy is learned and distinguished?

The 'derivation' meaning of *παραλογίζεσθαι* need not be insisted on. It is only "*delude*," as in the Epistle of St. James (i. 22). In an interesting note L. informs us that in Aristotle and Plato *πιθανολογία* ('probable argument,' or 'argument based on probability') is opposed to 'demonstration' (ἀπόδειξις), and bids us mark (in 1 Cor. ii. 4) phraseology in St. Paul which seems to have reference to this distinction of the philosophers. And indeed it is, to say the least of it, a curious coincidence. Here, however, πιθανολογία is not contrasted with exact proof, and bears unmistakably a sinister sense. Indeed, I believe it is sinister in both its elements, for πιθανός suggests plausibility, and λογία long-windedness. Therefore I render it 'specious talk.' These thinkers multiply words, and fair-sounding words which appear to have something in them, with singular dexterity. Therefore St. Paul would have the Colossians not forget their teacher's teacher, whose heart goes out to them in loving anxiety. In 'spirit' he is with them. The very remarkable language of 1 Cor. v. 3, 4 should be carefully compared. Here the 'in spirit' (his own spirit) might clearly mean little more than 'in thought.' There it must mean a good deal more: "you being gathered together *and my spirit*" undoubtedly conveys the sense of an interest so strong and clearly defined that it becomes all but equivalent to a presence palpable. The sense of such a 'presence,' unseen but none the less real, he wants to bring home to them now. The effect is intentionally heightened by the language which he employs in the very next clause. He is there. He rejoices. He actually *sees*. The order of χαίρων καὶ βλέπων is suggestive of *hysteron proteron*. It is due to the complex character of the thing which is seen. For all practical purposes it means simply "*joyfully seeing*." It must be the sight (nothing else) which brings the joy. *Τάξις* and *στερέωμα* are both military terms. St. Paul's interest in soldiering was developed by the experience of daily personal contact with Roman private soldiers. *Στερέωμα* in L.'s illustration appears to mean 'main body.' Here it obviously means 'solid front.' The statement, strong as it is, accords with the Apostle's normal manner. It will be noted how he passes on, after speaking of their 'doughty' faith, to suggest it well might be even doughtier than it is. At least it meant well; it desired to be strong and genuine; but it failed somewhat on the side of understanding. To Christ they wished to be loyal, but their conception of His Being was altogether inadequate. Still that was not their teacher's fault: it was they who had forgotten his teachings, or let them be overlaid with later accretions.

ii. 6, 7. "As then you were instructed about 'the Christ,' (that He is) Jesus, the LORD, (so) walk in Him; firmrooted (in Him) and evermore 'built up' in Him, and made firmer in 'the faith,'" (or "in your faith") "as you were taught (it); abounding therein, with thanksgiving." Cf. iv. 2 (in margin).

"*You were instructed.*" The Greek says, "*You received.*" Oral instruction is constantly represented by words which literally mean 'hand over,' 'take over.' To the ancient mind there was a something especially sacred and solemn in actual oral transmission. The opening of *v.* 6 I have made bold to expand a little. To begin with, "*You received the Christ*" is not exactly explicit to the English reader. "*The Christ*" (we must understand) is the subject or topic of instruction. Hence I have said "*you were instructed about. . . .*" The true teaching about Him centres on two fundamental dogmas. He is real 'man' (this truth is put forward before us by the human Name—the Name of the Incarnation). He is also real God (this latter is indicated, rather than stated, by the use of the title "*Lord,*" cf. Phil. ii. 11). The double truth is here enunciated with what is, for our minds, a bewildering brevity. Yet it all is there. Compare (before we pass on) the corresponding Ephesian section (Ephes. iv. 20, 21):

"But you have not so learned 'the Christ'; that is, if you heard about Him," (*not* 'listened to Him,' as our English version might suggest) "and were schooled (ἐδιδάχθητε) 'in Him,' even as truth" (perhaps, '*the* truth') "is in Jesus. . . ."

This again (it must be allowed) is not exactly easy. 'The Christ' (the whole doctrine of Him) is the subject matter of the 'learning'; the εἴγε introduces a 'proviso,' for the teaching may have failed on the part of the pupils. Καὶ ἐν αὐτῷ ἐδιδάχθητε is excessively hard to be sure of: I should say that it must mean "were taught *so as to be* 'in Him.'" But that is a large expansion. The verb (ἐδιδάχθητε) describes a process which may have taken time, but now is over and done with—in fact, their original pre-baptismal instruction.

Our Colossian passage (I think) contains more than the Ephesian one, though truly in fewer words. Still they should be studied side by side.

"*Walk in Him*" is another expression amazingly concise. It means (as I apprehend) 'live in the power of His faith, in union with His Person.'

"*Firmrooted*" (ἐρριζωμένοι) suggests really a foundation. The varying tenses of the Greek are hard to reproduce. The 'building up' and the 'growing firm' are present and 'continuous'; the 'firmrooted' is present and 'complete.' That is, it is genuinely 'perfect.' The dative may mean "*by* faith" or "*in* faith." For my part, I incline to the latter. It is their 'faith' which calls for greater vigour. There is the need of growth. In spite of my paraphrase I cannot be sure that "in *the faith,* as you were taught it" is the proper rendering. Observe the reiteration of the statement as to the absolute correctness of what they were taught at the first. Ἐν αὐτῇ, perhaps, suggests that τῇ πίστει means in 'faith' and not in 'the faith.'

As we pass on through the Epistle we shall find a constant insistence on the duty of thanksgiving. It is strange, and yet not strange, that the Apostle in his prison-house learned to know the need of this ever more and more. Other prisoners have also.

And now we must gird up our loins to face a long passage of great difficulty, and of very great importance. In the course of it we shall learn incidentally what the nature of the false teaching at Colossæ probably was.

ii. 8. "Oh! see that there shall be none who carries

you off as prey, by means of his 'philosophy' and vain deceit, following the traditions of men, following the 'rudimentary teaching of the world,' and not following Christ."

The word I have rendered by 'carry off as prey' is essentially invidious. It is exceedingly rare in literature. Once only in St. Paul, it does not recur again till very late. Heliodorus (a Thessalian Bishop, of *circ.* A.D. 390 it is thought) uses it in the sense 'kidnap': 'he it is who *kidnapped* my daughter' (*οὗτός ἐστιν ὁ τὴν ἐμὴν θυγάτερα συλαγωγήσας*), though whether the excellent man was speaking literally or metaphorically I am not in a position to tell. '*Kidnap*' is what it means here. Elsewhere (in 2 Tim. iii. 6) the Apostle describes the same sinister activities of misleading teachers by another figure, 'leading captive': "*Of these are they that creep* (*ἐνδύνοντες*, 'worm their way') *into houses and lead captive* (*αἰχμαλωτίζοντες*) *silly women* (*γυναικάρια*). . . ." Theosophists, and Christian Scientists and Spiritualists are (probably) all of them people whom he would have so described. They are, all of them, 'kidnappers.' With regard to *αἰχμαλωτίζοντες*, it is interesting to note that the less classical LXX form *αἰχμαλωτεύειν* is applied to Christ Himself, in connexion with Psalm lxxxviii. Otherwise the kingly word belonging to Christ, as the conqueror of souls, is here (and in 2 Corinthians) the magnificent *θριαμβεύειν*. That stands in impressive contrast to the mean and hateful *συλαγωγεῖν*, which describes 'hole and corner' intrigues.

Literally our first line means, 'Have a care there shall be none' (or, 'not be any') 'that kidnaps you. . . .' The form of the clause is 'modal.' It is equivalent to ὅπως μὴ ἔσται. The sentence is strangely constructed and on wholly non-classical lines. The expression διὰ τῆς φιλοσοφίας ("*using his philosophy*") is a quotation, so far at least as the term 'philosophy' goes, of the actual language of these persons. They called their strange views 'philosophy,' even as our Christian Scientists denominate their views 'science.' The reference is not to 'Philosophy,' so called, that is, Hellenic philosophy. Philo and Josephus employ the term of systems of religion, even of Judaism. The three contemporary Jewish sects are called by the latter 'three philosophies'; while the system of the Essenes is similarly called by the former. No doubt, then, the false teachers at Colossæ employed the same imposing appellation to describe their singular *farrago* of angelology, asceticism and what not. But St. Paul, without mincing matters, denominates it "*vain delusion*" (κενὴ ἀπάτη). In the three succeeding phrases he justifies his condemnation on three grounds. It is 'human' in origin; it is essentially 'elementary' (as being un-spiritual); in a word, it is *not* Christianity (however much it may claim to be so). It is not "*after Christ.*" Παράδοσις means no more than 'teaching'; strictly speaking, 'oral' teaching, but not so of necessity. The very curious expression τὰ στοιχεῖα τοῦ κόσμου ("*the rudiments of the world*") the writer has used before, in

Galatians iv. 3, 9. "*So we also, when we were children*" (literally, "babes," νήπιοι), "*were in subjection to* 'worldly rudiments,' *completely enslaved* (δεδουλωμένοι). . . ." These vigorous terms describe the pre-Christian religious stage; when something was known of God, but not very much; when religion consisted in externals, and not in the spiritual. In *v.* 9 below (Gal. iv.) the Apostle actually asks his Galatian converts whether, having once "*known God*" (through the coming of the Gospel), they propose to turn back again to the "*weak and worthless rudiments*" (ἀσθενῆ καὶ πτωχὰ στοιχεῖα). Now it is true that the people addressed are, for the more part, ex-heathen, but notice, that beyond a doubt the "*weak and worthless rudiments*" to which they were retrograding (for it was a real retrogression) is a phrase employed by St. Paul to cover what we call Judaistic teaching, circumcision and the like; for the believers in Galatia were indubitably exposed to "Judaistic" influences. Πτωχά he calls this elementary teaching (στοιχεῖα means 'a.b.c.') in contrast to the wealth and '*richness*' of the Gospel. Our English 'beggarly' is extremely inappropriate. The 'rudiments' are only 'beggarly' in so far as they are ineffectual. Here again, in the later Colossians, the old phrase reappears. It does not mean exactly the same thing, but it means the same sort of thing. It is still 'non-spiritual' and mainly 'external' (τοῦ κόσμου); it is still 'rudimentary,' fit only for 'babes' (στοιχεῖα). It masquerades as Christianity, and it is not. It is only the 'teaching *of men.'* Whereas Christianity is essentially a revelation, a 'mystery' indeed, as no other mystery is; as for this so-called 'philosophy,' it is the merest 'delusion' (as has been already said), and its condemnation lies in this, it departs from, gives up, CHRIST. The supreme truth as to Christ is that He is wholly God. Hence no other power is needed: He in Himself is all-sufficient. This great convincing truth sweeps away, as so many cobwebs, the vain imaginings of 'mediating angels.' They are left with no purpose to serve. The Incarnation accomplishes all. All the silly Colossian folks, who have been so artfully 'kidnapped,' had better make their way home, and rest in the grand simplicity of the one and only Gospel.

" . . . *Not after Christ*" (he says),

ii. 9. "for in Him dwells all the fulness of the Godhead bodily. . . ."

Here we have the "*bodily*" I desiderated above. Let us see how it is explained. 'Assuming a bodily form' (says L.), 'becoming incarnate.' Here lurks an ambiguity. Σωματικῶς becomes equivalent to '*having taken a body.*' Well, of course, it may be so. He would be a bold man, indeed, who should say it could not be. 'Σωματικῶς' (says L. again) 'is added to show that the Word . . . crowned His work by the Incarnation.' Yet all St. Paul is concerned with here is merely this, that Christ is *wholly God*: he is not for a moment concerned with His twofold Being, as 'Jesus' and as LORD (as we had it just now). The complete and utter 'Godhead' (θεότης) is what we want. Σωματικῶς, therefore, must mean "*bodily*," whether the word be found elsewhere in that sense or not. I learn with pleasure (from L.) that Jerome so interpreted it, "*nequaquam per partes.*" That is precisely what I want, 'altogether,' 'utterly.' If I am told it is unexampled, I point to the use of σῶμα below (in *v.* 17). That is bold enough in all conscience.

From the 'fulness' of Christ's Godhead flows a fulness for His people. The Church as a whole may be called πλήρωμα ("*a full thing*"), and separate believers are 'full,' so far as they may be 'full' (and that of necessity varies with the individual), in virtue of union with Him. Recall again St. John i. 16, "*and of His 'fulness' have we all of us received, and* χάριν ἀντὶ χάριτος," and Ephes. iii. 14-19, which embodies the Apostle's prayer for the Asiatic believers. He prays for their spiritual strengthening; he prays that Christ may 'take up His abode' (κατοικῆσαι τὸν Χριστόν), through faith, in their hearts; he prays that they may have power to apprehend (καταλαβέσθαι) "*with all the Saints*" the ineffable proportions, the unimaginable magnitude—of what, we are not told in so many words; but we conclude (from what follows), of the Love of Christ; and the conclusion of all is—the great end toward which all the supplication moves—"*that ye may be fulfilled unto all the fulness of God.*"

The ἵνα πληρωθῆτε there affords a correction to the πεπληρωμένοι here, and shows us we must understand it potentially, rather than actually. The point is that, if they are 'fulfilled,' the 'fulfilment' comes "*in Him.*" A consideration of this passage and that suggests that in Ephes. i. 23 the πληρουμένου is middle in voice: the Church is said to be His 'Body,' 'the *pleroma* of Him who *fulfils everything everywhere*'—that is to say, whatever real 'fulness' there may be, is all due to Him alone: the destiny of man, which is essentially 'spiritual,' can only be achieved by His sole means.

About the rendering of *v.* 10 I cannot feel confident. Either it means "*And you are 'in Him,' fulfilled*"—this is the way that L. would take it—or "*and your 'fulness'* (your fulfilment) *is in Him.*" The latter I believe to be right, with the proviso that St. Paul does not predicate this 'completeness' of all of them. It is the Church which is σεσωσμένος, the Church which is πεπληρωμένος, and not the individual.

Accordingly, let us render it:

ii. 10. "And in Him you are fulfilled" (notice, there is no stress on the 'you,' for in the Greek the personal pronoun is not expressed), "seeing He is the fountain-head of all authority and power."

Here once more I should hold that ὅς is equivalent to ὅσγε, so that the relative clause supplies the reason for the statement which precedes it. Ἀρχή ("authority") and ἐξουσία ("power") do not need to be discriminated in this case. The duplication of terms lends solemnity to the pronouncement.

Hereupon we come to teaching such as the

Apostle might have given in Galatians years before. It is a most urgent admonition against imagining there is virtue still in actual 'circumcision.' There were, then, people at Colossæ who erred even in this respect.

ii. 11. ". . . Aye, in Him you have been circumcised" (if 'circumcision' is what you seek) "with a circumcision supernatural, wherein you put off effectually the body's frailty, with the circumcision of Christ."

Circumcision is, in effect, a recognition by the worshipper of his liability to bestial passion; nay, even possibly a prophylactic, in some measure; but the recognition is of small value, and the remedial character of the rite (if any) is feeble. What man desiderates is to rise above the mere animal. This Christ (says St. Paul) achieves for him. His 'circumcision' is infinitely more than an outward ritual form. It is *ἀχειροποίητος*, literally, 'not made with hands,' but the word means a good deal more (as L. points out) to ears habituated to the Greek O.T. In our N.T. Scriptures it is found but thrice: in the statement of the 'false witnesses' as given in St. Mark:

"I will pull down this 'shrine' that is 'made with hands' and after three days I will build another 'not made with hands'" (St. Mark xiv. 58.)

(this certainly was never said by Christ: what He did say we have from St. John, chapter ii. 19); in 2 Cor. v. 1, where the Apostle tells his readers that if the 'earthly tabernacle' (the body that now is) be 'demolished,' there remains a building *ἀχειροποίητος* (this is the *σῶμα πνευματικόν* of 1 Cor. xv. 44), so that we shall not be left 'homeless'; and lastly, we have it here, not applied to a building at all, but used in the broadest sense. This circumcision is not 'human' but 'divine'; it comes from Christ, not Moses; it achieves the heart's desire; it frees man from the *σάρξ*. The 'natural' body remains; we have it all through our earthly life; but the *σάρξ* of it (all its lower elements) is eliminated, disappears. As St. Paul says, it is "*doffed*." The *σῶμα* of the *σάρξ* might be the 'substance of the *σάρξ*,' but I think it is not. The relation of the two genitives must remain, for us, undetermined. They might be in 'apposition,' "*the body, I mean the lower nature*," but I think it is more likely that the expansion really means 'the *σάρξ* of the *σῶμα*.' Only, why are the words in that order? The idea, at any rate, is clear enough. The 'body' (though not yet completely 'redeemed') remains: the passions go. They really and truly go, if a man continues "*in Christ*." This circumcision, this putting off of carnal frailty, is a thing of the past for the readers; therefore it is expressed in the aorist. The next verse passes on to show that it is to be identified with the rite of incorporation in Holy Baptism. Baptism contains, at the least, the 'potentiality' of such a deliverance. Always 'faith' lies in the background. So this potentiality may go unrealised. It is to be assumed that with some of those Colossians unrealised it was. But now they shall be reminded of their 'goodly heritage.'

ii. 12. "For you were buried with Him, in your Baptism, wherein also you were raised with Him through faith in the (mighty) working of God, Who raised Him from the dead. . . ."

The doctrine of this verse is plain enough, and needs no elucidation. The Apostle merely reminds them of the 'thing signified' (thanks, Dean Overall!) in that most essential sacrament; 'a death unto sin, and a new birth unto righteousness.' The 'burial' under the water is the pledge of effective 'death'; the 'rising again' is the symbol of the new '*pneumatic*' life. 'Baptism' in Holy Writ is usually *βάπτισμα,* when it stands for the Christian rite. Here we have *βαπτισμός*, a word which could hardly be used of an individual 'baptism'—for it is, perhaps, a 'process' word—though (*teste* L.) in Latin Fathers the words are often used indiscriminately. Here the phrase means "*in your baptising,*" that is, 'when they baptised you.'

Observe the prodigious emphasis the Apostle lays on 'faith.' *Διὰ τῆς πίστεως* he says. Compare the well-known words of Romans x. 9:

"For if thou shalt confess the word with thy lips (declaring) JESUS is LORD (ὅτι κύριος Ἰησοῦς), and shalt believe in thy heart, that God raised Him from the dead (ὅτι ὁ Θεὸς ἤγειρεν αὐτὸν ἐκ νεκρῶν), thou shalt be saved (σωθήσῃ)."

The three verses that follow next (ii. 13-15) must be carefully compared with a passage in Ephesians displaying a considerable degree of verbal resemblance, though the general drift is different. I think it might be well, before we approach the text before us, briefly to refer to this. The passage is Ephes. ii. 11-18. The writer bids his readers remember that they were Gentiles once, called "uncircumcised" by the Jews; that they were estranged from Israel and all Israel's 'promises.' But now the prophetic word (Isaiah lvii. 19) has been accomplished in them; being 'afar' they have been made 'near.' Hitherto I have been giving the bare outline of *vv.* 11, 12, 13. It is now that we come upon the 'verbal resemblance.' Jew and Gentile have been made 'one,' the old enmity (typified by the barrier in the Temple, beyond which no Gentile might pass) has been actually 'killed.'

But let me paraphrase the sacred text.

> ". . . For He is our Peace,
> that hath made the two one
> and hath broken down the dividing wall
> of the barrier,
> the (old) enmity,
> in His flesh,"

(that is, by His incarnation and its sequel)

> "having abolished the Law of the commands
> in ordinances
> (τὸν νόμον τῶν ἐντολῶν ἐν δόγμασι καταργήσας)
> that He might make (κτίσῃ) the two
> in Himself
> into one 'new man,'
> making peace;
> and might reconcile
> both parties (τοὺς ἀμφοτέρους)
> in one body"

(I apprehend this '*body*' is His Church, in which are united Jew and Gentile)

"to God,
by means of His Cross,
having killed by it (ἐν αὐτῷ)
the (old) enmity . . .
for by His means we have,
Jew and Gentile
(οἱ ἀμφότεροι),
our access
in one spirit
to the Father."
(Ephes. ii. 14-18, omitting 17.)

It will be seen that here the writer is dwelling on a very definite topic—the union in one body of Jew and Gentile 'in Christ,' achieved by virtue of His Cross, which has definitely abolished all that of old combined to keep them apart. The special point of connexion between the language here and there lies in the reference to "law." In Ephesians this "law" *of* "*commands and ordinances*" (τῶν ἐντολῶν ἐν δόγμασιν) is definitely Moses' Law, no doubt, with the ordinance of circumcision included, though that was pre-Mosaic. It is regarded plainly as being of the nature of a division between Jew and Gentile. Its 'abolition' (καταργήσας) is set forth as a prerequisite of the new and happy union of all mankind achieved by Christ. All this is simple enough.

When we turn to Colossians again, we find law spoken of allusively rather than directly; but the reference does not appear till the writer has decisively included Jews also in his purview. This will be seen when we turn to the text:

ii. 13-15. "Yes, you that were dead in your transgressions and your 'carnal uncircumcision'—you, I say, God has 'quickened' together with Christ, and has 'forgiven' *us* all our transgressions, having 'washed out' the 'note of hand,' that was against us, which stood in our way with its decrees; aye, He has taken it clean away, having nailed it to His Cross; stripping bare the principalities and powers, He has openly paraded them, leading them in triumph through *It*."

In the opening of this section St. Paul addresses his readers as Gentiles. They were 'sinners,' they were 'dead'; they were literally 'uncircumcised'; but this uncircumcision of fact was only a 'symbol' (as L. affirms) of the condition of unrestrained animalism in which they lived. Now, by God's great mercy, they share the new life of the Risen Redeemer; share it now 'in part,' shall share it fully hereafter. God 'raised' Him, and with Him them. Their sins are all 'forgiven.' The delightful term by which this forgiveness is here expressed (*χαρισάμενος*, literally 'having made us a present of our sins') is a Lucano-Pauline term. For a characteristic instance see 2 Cor. ii. 7. It accords with Christ's own conception of sins as 'debts.' "*Forgive us our debts*," Christ taught His own to pray (*ἀφὲς ἡμῖν τὰ ὀφειλήματα*, St. Matt. vi. 12). That is precisely what Our Father has done with a truly royal bounty (*χαρισάμενος ἡμῖν πάντα τὰ παραπτώματα*, "having freely 'given' us all our sins"). And this magnifical bounty touches Jew as well as Gentile: it is St. Paul's as well as theirs. For here (it will be noted), as often in St. Paul, the "*you*" changes into an "*us.*" It is just this inclusion of the Jew which makes it possible for the writer to go on as he does. Our sins are represented not merely as 'debts'; by a very vigorous figure it is said that there stands against us an 'I.O.U.' or 'note of hand.' Our 'debts' are open and acknowledged: our own 'writ of hand' is against us: there is no possible appeal. Only one thing will save us, the cancelling of that document which witnesses to the 10,000 talents, the inconceivable sum, in which we remain 'indebted' to God in heaven.

But this 'cancelling' is achieved. Sin is all 'blotted out,' 'washed out.' It might have been merely 'crossed out,' with a great 'X' drawn across it. But it is far better than that; the whole thing is obliterated; it is as though it had never been. It would seem that ancient ink was more easy to wash out than the ink of nowadays. Old documents were often so treated and the paper used over again. We have mention (from A.D. 140) of a χειρόγραφον—a 'bond' such as is contemplated here—χωρὶς ἀλείφατος καὶ ἐπιγραφῆς 'neither *washed out* nor written over.' The reference will be found in Dr. Milligan's little book of *Selections of Greek Papyri*, Introduction, p. xxii. This "*bond*" of ours is "*washed out.*" The grammar of *v.* 14 has not unnaturally caused trouble to commentators. I believe that τοῖς δόγμασιν belongs to what follows, and therefore have rendered it as though it ran ὃ ἦν ὑπενάντιον ἡμῖν τοῖς δόγμασιν ("*which stood in our way, with its decrees*, or rules"). Τὸ χειρόγραφον τοῖς δόγμασιν could only stand if (contrary to Pauline usage) it had to be taken on the principle of 'instalment' familiar to readers of the Classics, as equivalent to τὸ καθ' ἡμῶν τοῖς δόγμασι χειρόγραφον. Take it as you will, the absence of a preposition with δόγμασιν is very awkward. It will be observed that in Ephes. ii. 15 there is a preposition.

But, what is this χειρόγραφον, this 'bond,' that stands against us, figuring the full extent of our debts, our obligations, as against GOD? It would seem in the end to be the Law—the Jewish Law, to which the nation had given, in the ratification of the Covenant at Sinai, and in the ceremony of Ebal and Gerizim, a very solemn adhesion. They, at least, were bound to fulfil it, and they neither had done so, nor ever could so do. And the ἡμῖν just above (χαρισάμενος ἡμῖν) undoubtedly includes Jews, for it includes St. Paul himself. As for δόγματα, we may be content to believe that it covers the definite 'rules' of the Law. The curious Greek interpretation, mentioned by L. (that the δόγματα are 'Gospel Precepts'), has nothing to recommend it. Our context and Ephes. ii. 15 are decisive for the meaning 'rules' or 'decrees.' As for the Gentiles, if they had no 'law,' they had, at least, a conscience (for God had not "*left Himself without witness*"); that is, what *we* should call a 'conscience'; and that for them discharged the function which the Law discharged for Israel. Every one remembers how in Romans the Apostle has argued that all mankind alike are guilty before God. This obliteration of acknowledged 'guilt,' for Jew and Gentile too, is first figured as the cancelling of a bond by actual washing out. Anon the writer changes the figure and represents Christ as carrying the incriminating document with Him upon His Cross. He "*has taken it right away* (ἦρκεν ἐκ τοῦ μέσου) *and nailed it*" (or "*by nailing it*"; we cannot tell which) "*to His Cross.*" There, to the Cross, His enemies 'nailed' Him. And He took with Him the burden of accumulated human guilt—the 'bond' not of you and me, but of all mankind. That too was 'nailed' to the Cross. St. Paul says, *He* nailed it! It is the thing foreshadowed in Isaiah liii.: it is the truth plainly stated in 1 Peter ii. 24. "*Who Himself 'carried up' in His body our sins upon 'the tree,' that having died to our sins*" (what an intensely Pauline phrase!) "*we might live to righteousness*" (τὰς ἁμαρτίας ἡμῶν αὐτὸς ἀνήνεγκεν ἐν τῷ σώματι αὐτοῦ ἐπὶ τὸ ξύλον).

Some folks cannot see their way to believe in 'forgiveness of sins.' Yet the Church most plainly teaches it, herein following Holy Writ; and I think a good many people would hold with me, that if you strike out that article from the Creed, you will have largely emptied the Gospel for the ordinary man of value and effectiveness. It is the thing we want most of all. Anyhow, I rejoice in the thought that St. Paul teaches it unflinchingly.

But we have not yet done with the Cross, the supreme instrument of Christ's triumph. It has achieved a great deal more than the cancelling of old sin. It carries with it the promise of a new great power of life. For why? It has been the final 'despoiling' of the unseen powers of evil. Christ has (by it) 'stripped,' stripped bare, the "*principalities and powers.*" Now, as for these, we feel fairly sure, on the strength of Ephesians vi., that they must be the powers wherewith the believer has to 'wrestle.'[1] "*Our* πάλη" (says St. Paul) "*is not with mere 'flesh and blood'*" (that is, with human enemies—if it were, it would not be so hard) "*but with principalities, but with powers, but with the world-potentates of this 'darkness,' but with the 'spiritualities,' of wickedness 'in the heavenlies'*" (ἀλλὰ πρὸς τὰς ἀρχάς, πρὸς τὰς ἐξουσίας, πρὸς τοὺς κοσμοκράτορας τοῦ σκότους τούτου, πρὸς τὰ πνευματικὰ τῆς πονηρίας ἐν τοῖς ἐπουρανίοις, Ephes. vi. 12). That last phrase, it must be admitted, is sufficiently awe-inspiring. 'Spiritualities of wickedness'—that is terrifying enough! But, ἐν τοῖς ἐπουρανίοις! What shall we make of that? At least, it is very certain that to St. Paul our 'ghostly enemy,' or, rather, 'our ghostly enemies' (a very host of them) were real foes indeed. But the text will bring us comfort. These foes have been 'stripped bare' by Christ. Said our Lord Jesus Christ, when on earth, "*but when a stronger than he shall come upon him and overcome him, he taketh from him his 'whole armour,' wherein his trust*

[1] But see Introduction, p. 20.

*lay* (ἐφ' ῇ ἐπεποίθει), *and divideth up his spoils.*' Moreover, He also indicated that His last and final bout with the Prince of Darkness was the hour of His Passion. In the Garden, on the Cross, the decisive encounter took place, and because He stooped very low — see Philippians and its triumphant declaration—therefore He rose very high.

Think of two sayings in our Gospels: St. Luke xxii. 53, "*This is your hour and the 'power of darkness'*" (αὕτη ἐστὶν ὑμῶν ἡ ὥρα—the Lord is addressing earthly foes, but others are in His mind —καὶ ἡ ἐξουσία τοῦ σκότους); and that of St. John, "*the Prince of 'the world' cometh*" (καὶ ἐν ἐμοὶ οὐκ ἔχει οὐδέν) (xiv. 30).

L. calls this interpretation (which has the authority, on his own evidence, of St. Jerome in its favour) 'a common error of interpretation.' He seems to be of opinion that ἀπεκδυσάμενος should mean 'having stripped *himself*' (*se*). But of course it should be *sibi*. As the judicious German said, the directly reflexive middle is 'very rare.' Therefore let us assume the indirect, "*having stripped for Himself*," that is, "*having succeeded in totally stripping*" (the double form of the ἀπό and the ἐκ L. properly insists on) "*the 'powers' and 'principalities.'*" With regard to ἐν παρρησίᾳ, L. would render it 'boldly,' but how can one 'parade' a conquered person 'boldly'? It does not need courage to do that—when his 'armour' (ἐφ' ῇ ἐπεποίθει) is wholly and totally removed! No (as he says himself), 'the idea of publicity may sometimes be connected with the word as a secondary notion.' Therefore, let us follow it here. *Traduxit confidenter* says the Vulgate: let us rather say *traduxit palam. Traduxit* ("*He paraded them*") is certainly what we want as the meaning of the verb.

Θριαμβεύειν is a rare word. In N.T. it comes but twice, and both times in St. Paul; here, and in 2 Cor. ii. 14. In the latter place our 'Revised' has corrected the old error of A.V. "*Leadeth us in triumph*" it reads in place of "*causeth us to triumph*," a sense which is nowhere in evidence. The whole context of the passage is full of the sense of suffering, and the Apostle pictures himself as a 'captive' in Christ's train—not 'triumphing,' but "*led in triumph*," wherever his Master wills. The same sense (unless I err) is found in the passage before us. The person over whom one celebrates a 'triumph' (a 'triumph' such as Romans loved) may be the object of the verb, or the things (and, presumably, persons) exhibited in such triumph. In view of the ἐδειγμάτισεν I think there can be little doubt that the latter is the right sense here. St. Paul is with St. John decisively in this matter. Both recognise that Our Lord has wholly conquered sin, and the powers that make for sin. St. Paul pictures his belief in the phrases we have before us. St. John places on the lips of the Conqueror Himself the all-sufficient statement, Θαρσεῖτε· ἐγὼ νενίκηκα τὸν κοσμόν, "*Fear not: I have overcome the world*"—where 'the world' stands for a good deal more than the term conveys to us. It covers all that is in opposition to God's Will; all the 'powers' and 'principalities' which lord it in 'this darkness.'

And, if this indeed be so, the believers at Colossæ must not burden and trouble their minds with little things, with trivial rules. It would be an absurdity. Accordingly, we read on:

ii. 16, 17. "Let not then any take you to task in regard to eating and drinking, or in respect of a feast or a new moon or a sabbath; which things are a (mere) shadow of '*the things to come,*' whereas Christ is '*the substance.*'"

It is well known that apart from the Naziritic vow the Law of Moses did not concern itself with drinking. The rules about 'things to eat' were very definite, some of them applying to all time, some only to certain sacred seasons. The rules applying to the former class were definitely abrogated by Our Lord Jesus Christ Himself. Religion no longer has anything at all to do with what one eats, or does not eat. Compare Romans xiv. 17. If we do not lay much stress on the phrase *καὶ ἐν πόσει*, all the rest of the language here falls within the Jewish Law. And it is desirable (considering the context) so to limit the sense for the present. Later on we shall be face to face with a more developed asceticism. The 'shadow' and the 'substance' point to the Law in its typical and symbolic aspects. 'Unclean meats' are merely 'shadow': the 'unleavened bread' of the Passover is merely 'shadow': the Paschal Lamb itself is merely 'shadow.' These things, one and all, belong to the age of preparation, what is called in other places "*the time that is*" (ὁ καιρὸς ὁ ἐνεστώς). Now, however, in the coming of the New Dispensation, all this σκιά is banished for good. We now enjoy the substance, the solid reality of which it was the promise. Was there a feast? was there a 'new moon'? was there a 'Sabbath'? It is all fulfilled in Christ. For the terms employed here by the Apostle, the 'shadow' (σκιά) and 'the things to come' (τὰ μέλλοντα), we must compare the language of Hebrews. In that Epistle we have (viii. 5) "*people who serve with a copy and a shadow of the things in heaven*" (ὑποδείγματι καὶ σκιᾷ λατρεύουσιν τῶν ἐπουρανίων)—I say 'with' because I believe the dative to be modal, expressing rather *how* they serve, than *what* they serve. The 'heavenly things' in that passage correspond more or less with 'the things to come' here. In another place we find both our terms standing side by side. It is in Hebrews x. 1. "*For the Law having a shadow of good things to come and not the things as they actually are*" (τὴν εἰκόνα τῶν πραγμάτων). The correspondence is very close, and the points of view, moreover, are unusually near. For here St. Paul is regarding (as he does not very frequently) Mosaic ordinances as prophecies of Christ. They are σκιά; He is σῶμα. As the reflection is to the thing reflected, so are they compared with Him. All the meaning of them, all the reality of them, is concentrated in Him. Where He is, they lose at once all significance and value. That is why the

Colossians must not let any 'criticise' (κρινέτω) them in regard to such matters. For these things are one and all just 'things indifferent.' The reality has come; the time for 'shadows' is over.

In the paraphrase above I have made bold to say "*Whereas Christ is the substance.*" This, apart from all forms of words, is clearly the Apostolic meaning. I take it, we may fairly render what he does say, something like this, "*Whereas the substance lies with Christ.*" Literally it runs, "*while the substance is Christ's.*" Meanwhile it was something more than a merely Mosaic 'legalism' from which the Colossians were suffering. This will soon emerge from the context. In Romans xiv. and in Galatians iv. the Apostle had dealt already with such 'unspiritual' weakness, and had laid down the great principle upon which abstinence from meat and drink, and the observance of holy days, must necessarily rest (Rom. xiv. 6). Here things have plainly gone further. Not merely were there people who said, 'A believer must be a vegetarian,' 'A believer must drink no wine'—things we have often heard said since; whereas the actual truth is that a believer in such matters should be guided by his own conscience—there were people who counselled the adoption of views even less reconcilable with Christian verity.

The next verse, however, presents many difficulties in language and reading, and it would be well to say something about them before passing on to consider paraphrase and interpretation. The difficulties of one kind and another gather round three elements in the sentence: (1) the verb *καταβραβεύειν*; (2) the phrase *θέλων ἐν ταπεινοφροσύνῃ*; (3) the clause *ἃ ἑώρακεν* (or, *ἃ μὴ ἑώρακεν*) *ἐμβατεύων.* Let something first be said about each of these.

With regard to (1), the perplexity lies in the exceeding rareness of the word. L. quotes it from a (probably fictitious) 'document' inserted in the text of Demosthenes against Meidias, p. 544. The words there are 'and we' (the witnesses, that is, whose names are given above) 'are well aware that for this reason Strato was *unjustly condemned* by Meidias's action and in violation of all right disenfranchised' (*ὑπὸ Μειδίου καταβραβευθέντα καὶ . . . ἀτιμωθέντα*). The reader is to understand that Meidias brought an action against Strato, in which (it is insinuated) he achieved by unfair means the unhappy man's condemnation and consequent loss of civil rights. All that emerges from this instance of the word is that it need not necessarily have anything to do with 'prizes' at all. It really means to 'umpire down,' that is to say, to wrong a person by an unjust decision as umpire. A corresponding *παραβραβεύειν* is actually found in Plutarch, used of an umpire who gives the prize to the wrong competitor. Perhaps *καταβραβεύειν* here means no more than to 'cheat,' but it *may* mean 'rob of a prize,' as L. says. In any case the 'race' metaphor is not very clearly in evidence.

With regard to (2), let it be said that sometimes in LXX (though not very often) *θέλειν ἐν* is used for to have pleasure or delight in. The usage is rather curiously sporadic. Hatch's Concordance affords five instances in the six Books of the Kings (including Chronicles), and three in the Psalms. If we suppose this to be the usage here (which Dr. Hort doubts, observing that St. Paul's style, 'except, of course, in quotations, is singularly free from crude Hebraisms,' *Notes on Select Readings*, p. 126), we must translate 'taking delight in humility.' In that case it would be desirable to regard *ἐν ταπεινοφροσύνῃ καὶ θρησκείᾳ τῶν ἀγγέλων* as one complete phrase, embodying a single idea: that idea would 'be (taking delight) in a self-humbling subservience to angels.' *Ταπεινοφροσύνη*, it is true, mainly bears a favourable sense. It is a virtue, not a vice. Here, however, it may incline to the significance it bore to the ordinary Greek ear. For if *ταπεινοφροσύνη* in Christian writings, for the most part, bears a good sense, *θρησκεία* (from the very root meaning of it, for it deals with the external) tends rather to an ill one (as Bishop Lightfoot says and shows). Dr. Hort, however, thinks that *θέλων* by itself can have no satisfactory meaning; that *θέλων ἐν* is non-Pauline; that *ταπεινοφροσύνη* could hardly be read in an ill sense without warning. Therefore he inclines to suspect some latent corruption. It may be that for *θέλων ἐν ταπεινοφροσύνῃ* we should read *ἐν ἐθελοταπεινοφροσύνῃ*. This would mean 'by a show of humility,' which would make very excellent sense.

The clause *ἃ ἑώρακεν ἐμβατεύων* is so exceedingly puzzling that (assuming it to be original) it was very early altered to the reading of the *textus receptus*, ἃ μὴ ἑώρακεν ἐμβατεύων ('intruding on what he has not seen'). Both Lightfoot and Hort in this place have suggested emendations. The former puts forward αἰώρᾳ κενεμβατεύων. The verb κενεμβατεύειν is not indeed found elsewhere; however, κενεμβατεῖν is. Therefore, with regard to the participle, we need feel no difficulty. Αἰώρα seems to denote some mechanical contrivance—a 'swing,' or the like. This suggestion is less attractive than that of Dr. Hort. He (following Dr. C. Taylor) would read ἀέρα κενεμβατεύων ('idly treading upon air'). If emendations are to be the order of the day, μετέωρα κενεμβατεύων is just conceivable. In any case the conception is of persons who idly talk of matters entirely beyond their ken, and that with meaningless and idle verbiage.[1]

[1] In the *Athenæum* for Jan. 25, 1913, there appeared a highly interesting contribution from Sir W. M. Ramsay entitled 'The Ancient Mysteries and their Relation to St. Paul.' Discoveries have been made, says the learned Professor, 'regarding the Mysteries celebrated at the great religious centres of Asia Minor under the later Roman Empire.' In one sanctuary, that of Mên at Antioch, was discovered a large Hall apparently used for Initiation. In it was an *impluvium* thought to have been used for a baptismal rite. The baptism was of a slighter kind than that at Eleusis, which was by immersion. This baptism (which took place before the image of the god) the Professor thinks was designed to 'outdo' the Christian rite. Inscriptions have also been found at a place called Notion, identified by Ramsay with Colophon. Inquirers, it appears, were sometimes 'initiated.' In connexion with these initiations the word ἐμβατεύειν twice occurs. In one case it is said of two inquirers, μυηθέντες, ἐνεβάτευσαν, of another that παραλαβών, τὰ μυστήρια ἐνεβάτευσεν. Plainly the word ἐμβατεύειν was technical in the Mysteries. These instances (he holds), though the meaning of the word is 'obscure,' confirm the reading of our text in Col. ii. 18. His conjectural interpretation is that the phrase meant "to put foot on the threshold," *i.e.* enter on the new life of the initiated. This seems likely enough. I should be tempted

We are now in a position to discuss a paraphrase. There are plainly a number of possibilities.

We might start with:

ii. 18. "Let no one *beat you down*, for all his will (to do so), by means of a humble-seeming subservience to angels. . . ."

(This would be an endeavour to cope with an independent θέλων.)

Or, again, we might read:

"Let no one *cheat* you, by taking delight in a self-humiliating subservience to angels."

Or, once more, following Hort:

"Let no one cheat you with a specious seeming humility and subservience to angels."

Plainly it cannot be very easy to come to a confident conclusion with regard to the metaphor involved in καταβραβευέτω, nor yet as to the reading to be followed in the phrase that comes next after. However, there were undoubtedly persons who averred that they displayed a more becoming humility by approaching angelic beings in place of approaching Christ directly and immediately. The Apostle obviously pours scorn upon those

---

to interpret simply 'pass in' or 'pass on.' It appears to me to represent the entering on a lower 'degree,' a stage before ἐποπτεύειν. For my own part, I should still hold that St. Paul uses in a plain and everyday sense a word which afterwards perhaps became technical in the Mysteries. It is very difficult to read any technical sense into St. Paul's words. He seems to be using an ordinary word in an ordinary way. Ramsay's suggestion is that a *mystes* had perturbed the Colossian Church by introducing the unspiritual teachings of the Mysteries, 'what *he had seen* there.' But I doubt.

This reference I owe to the kindness of Sir Herbert Thompson.

'blind guides' in the two vehement clauses that follow. On the one hand, he represents them as:

Either (1) 'dwelling on what (they declare) they have seen.'

Or (2) 'intruding upon things beyond their vision.'

Or (3) 'embarking upon airy nothings' (if we follow either conjecture).

Upon the other, he roundly affirms that they are 'puffed up without ground (εἰκῇ) by their gross and material reason' (1 Cor. viii. 1). It would seem that such persons claimed to be guided in some especial sense by what they themselves called *νοῦς* (intelligence). For the unillumined reason the Apostle feels nothing but scorn, when it intrudes upon alien spheres. The 'reason of the flesh' is wholly unable to cope with the 'deep things' of the 'Spirit.'

To sum up, accordingly, he regards such people as dangerous, as self-deluded, as led astray by a vain conceit that is based on a merely fanciful knowledge. They cast aside realities (though there is only *One* Reality) to grasp after idle shadows. To follow them means to lose all.

But the time has surely come to make up our minds some way.

I incline, then, to paraphrase thus:

ii. 18. ". . . Let no one *disinherit* you, for all his eagerness, by pretended humility in adoration of angels. He is intruding upon spheres beyond his range of vision: he is filled with a vain conceit through his unillumined imaginings. Moreover, he does not hold fast the HEAD. . . ."

'The Head,' of course, is Christ, as in the Ephesian parallel. This paraphrase, it will be seen, is highly conservative. It even accepts the *μή*. That has considerable MS. authority, and for my part I would hold that, if there be early corruption, that corruption might have included the extrusion of the negative. Happily, it matters exceedingly little what special reading, or even correction, we choose to follow. Nothing can obscure the facts: first, that these false teachers and their followers paid worship (in some form) to 'angels'; secondly, that in doing so they affected (or might have affected) to display a more seemly attitude on the part of mortals face to face with the Infinite Majesty.

Verse 19 recalls at once a parallel in Ephesians. It would be well to consider that before making up our minds about the words before us. In Ephesians there are two verses (iv. 15, 16) corresponding to our one.

Here are the words of the parallel:

". . . but maintaining the truth in love (ἀληθεύοντες ἐν ἀγάπῃ) *may grow* to Him in all things (αὐξήσωμεν εἰς αὐτὸν τὰ πάντα), Who is *the* HEAD, (even) Christ, *from Whom the whole Body* nicely adjusted *and compacted* (συναρμολογούμενον καὶ συμβιβαζόμενον)"—although it is a 'body' its growth is set before us in terms derived from stonemasons' work—"*thanks to every joint* of its furnishing (διὰ πάσης ἁφῆς τῆς ἐπιχορηγίας) by right discharge of function in every single part (κατ' ἐνέργειαν ἐν μέτρῳ ἑνὸς ἑκάστου μέρους) achieves *the body's growth* (τὴν αὔξησιν τοῦ σώματος ποιεῖται) unto its own upbuilding in love (εἰς οἰκοδομὴν αὐτοῦ ἐν ἀγαπῃ)." (I have italicised all phrases here that are closely similar.)

A broad consideration of this sentence will show that the 'Body' is regarded coincidently as a 'body' and a 'structure.' Both figures have their own peculiar values; neither covers all the facts. A building is built, *i.e.* derives its increase, from a something outside itself. A body, on the other hand, 'grows.' The Christian Church has its growth at once in itself and not in itself! It depends how you regard it.

If I were asked what I myself considered to be the most difficult point in that sentence (as in the Colossian one) I should say, without hesitation, the *ἐξ οὗ*. Does the preposition represent 'dependence' (as it might have been 'hanging on Whom')? or does it represent 'the Head' as the primal 'source' of all fruitful development? In Colossians (unless I err) the latter is the more likely: about the Ephesian usage I cannot feel nearly so confident. Colossians too does not present us with interwoven metaphors. Our body is only a body, and is wholly described in terms appropriate to a body. Yet one of them is dubious in regard to its signification. That is the word *ἁφαί*, of which (as the Dean of Wells has shown) Bishop Lightfoot probably took too narrow a view. He held that its root idea is that of 'contact,' but *ἁφή* has many senses which are far removed from that. The noun is a verbal one, and has relations to *ἅπτειν* (in more than one sense of the active), and also to *ἅπτεσθαι* (which supplies a wholly new string of ideas connected with 'attachment'). Yet we can only guess its meaning here, being sure that it is a term derived from the surgeon's vocabulary. Our verse, then, I would English as follows:

ii. 19. ". . . and not holding fast the Head, from Whom all the body—thanks to its joints and ligatures—deriving its support and its increasing strength grows with the growth of God."

The words διὰ τῶν ἁφῶν καὶ συνδέσμων I have placed in a parenthesis, because I want to emphasise the immediate dependence of the all-important participles ἐπιχορηγούμενον and συμβιβαζόμενον upon the ἐξ οὗ. The joints and the ligatures perform their part in making the body one, in keeping it together. Its nourishment, its increasing strength, depend on a something greater. They wholly derive from the Head.

"*The growth of God*" is a phrase which admits of several interpretations. Here I believe the meaning is, 'the growth which is after God's mind'; 'grows as God would have it grow.' Remember that in Ephesians this growth is essentially "*in love.*"

The decay of faith at Colossæ is exhibited in the practices which are coming into vogue. A failure to appreciate the real meaning of Christ on the part of Christian men has issued in a tendency to various ascetic usages, not very clearly defined. So the Apostle indignantly asks:

ii. 20-23. "Oh! if you died with Christ and gave *up the worldly rudiments*, why as though living in the worldly sphere do you *make rules for yourselves* (such as) 'Touch not, taste not, handle not'—(rules having to do with things) all of which pass away in the using, following ordinances and teachings which are (nothing more than) human? Such rules have a *show of wisdom*, dealing ruthlessly with the body through self-imposed austerities and (voluntary) humiliation, but are not of any value as against sensual indulgence."

We have already had in the chapter mention of the believer's mystical death and mystical resurrection associated with Baptism (see *vv.* 11, 12). Such teaching reproduces the well-known doctrines already put forth in Galatians and in Romans, not to mention other letters. See especially Gal. ii. 19, 20, and Rom. vii. 4-6, though it runs through all the Epistles. This mystical death is past: therefore it is naturally expressed in the aorist ἀπεθάνετε. The ἀπό is, of course, 'pregnant': therefore in English we must represent it by a definite 'verbal' clause. The expression "the worldly rudiments," though obscure to the English reader, is quite distinct in its meaning. It comes twice in Galatians iv. (*vv.* 3 and 9) and twice in this one chapter. It implies a rudimentary form of religion consisting mainly in external rites. See on *v.* 8 above. With the κόσμος (the material order) the Christian man, as such, has nothing to do. He is in it, but not of it. He belongs to another sphere and lives on another plane. His life (as we shall see) is "*hid with Christ in God.*" As for δογματίζεσθε, it is hard to tell whether it should be middle or passive. In the Greek O.T. the passive is found in several places; the middle nowhere. But, if this verb be passive, it is not after the pattern of the O.T. instances. Their subjects are 'rules' of one sort or another, not persons. Therefore I incline to think it stands for *δογματίζετε ἑαυτοῖς δόγματα* ('rule for yourselves rules'). We have examples of such 'rules' (any other interpretation of the words is blankly impossible) in the three prohibitions which follow: "Do not lay hold of (this or that)! Do not taste (the other thing)! Do not touch!" As L. very justly says, *ἅψῃ* is stronger than *θίγῃς*. But I have kept the familiar rendering because it matters little, and the words are for us inevitable. No doubt the Apostle had in his thought when he penned the passage the well-known teaching of Our Lord contained in the Gospel story. In the seventh chapter of St. Mark (1-23) the Lord deals in His trenchant way with Pharisaic 'tradition.' Found fault with because His disciples ate their bread with unwashed hands, He quotes Isaiah's words:

> "This people honoureth Me with their lips,
> but their heart is far away from Me;
> in vain do they worship Me,
> teaching doctrines, human ordinances"

(*διδάσκοντες διδασκαλίας, ἐντάλματα ἀνθρώπων*, which is not exact LXX). (Isaiah xxix. 13.)

Thereupon He proceeds to carry the warfare into His opponents' country by denouncing the way in which they employed the solemn word *Corban*, so as by a legal fiction to cancel filial obligation. "*Any benefit you have gotten by me is (henceforth) Corban*" (ran the formula); that is to say, by a mock dedication of his property, the ungrateful son released himself from the duty of supporting his father. Of this most unrighteous proceeding Our Lord declared, "*You make void the word of God by your tradition*" (ἀκυροῦντες τὸν λόγον τοῦ Θεοῦ τῇ παραδόσει ὑμῶν), the reference being primarily to the fifth of the ten great 'Words.' To this Teaching is appended in the Gospel the famous παραβολή (that is, 'figurative saying'), "*The things which come out of a man, it is they that defile him*" (St. Mark vii. 15). In His own interpretation of this 'parable' there occur the well-known words (about the thing which passes into the man), "*It cannot defile him, because it goes not into his heart*" (the seat of his spiritual life) "*but into his belly, and passes out again in natural course*"; whereto is appended in our oldest MSS. the brief and pithy comment, "*And He made clean all meats*" (καθαρίζων πάντα τὰ βρώματα). Now the fact that in St. Paul there is a similar statement about 'meats,' and other material things, that they all "*perish in the using*" and thereby proclaim their connexion not with the spiritual but the material, and the further fact that he cites (in briefer form) the very same words of the prophet, amount almost to proof positive that he is speaking with clear remembrance of what His Master had said. At the same time we must bear in mind that on the lips of Christ the 'human ordinances' only referred to oral additions made since to the written Law; whereas, plainly, the Apostle would extend its meaning much further.

For him the bondage of 'Law' has wholly ceased: the new era, the era of the spirit, is definitely begun. For Christ it was not. Indeed it could not begin till His great work was accomplished. When He had died, when He had been raised again, when He had sent the Holy Spirit, *then* the New Order truly began! Our Lord lived as a Jew, in no way discarding the Law, only disregarding the superstructure of intricate regulations which the Doctors had piled upon it.

To return once more to the text, it is not easy to supply the prohibiting verbs 'touch,' 'taste' and 'handle' with their appropriate objects. Ἅψῃ has been thought by some to refer to sexual intercourse (cf. 1 Cor. vii. 1); but this is distinctly unlikely. L. is doubtless right in declaring the reference is partly to re-enactments of Mosaic Law, partly to 'Essene' exaggerations in the direction of asceticism. He mentions such details as the avoidance of oil and wine; the abstinence from flesh meat; the scrupulous care to shun any contact with inferior persons. But (though 'taste not' affords no puzzle) it is difficult to be certain what sort of things might not be 'touched' with the lightest kind of contact (*μὴ θίγῃς*), what things might not be 'handled' (*μὴ ἅψῃ*). The phrase from Isaiah which follows is not exactly cited. There it runs *διδάσκοντες ἐντάλματα ἀνθρώπων καὶ διδασκαλίας* ("*teaching human ordinances and teachings*"). The change is perhaps significant. The prophet does not contemplate Mosaic Law at all. That is, for him, the 'Word of God.' St. Paul's modification seems to cover specific Mosaic 'rules' with 'human' amplifications, such as Judaic ascetics delighted in.

Λόγον ἔχοντα σοφίας is rendered by L. 'having a reputation for wisdom.' Maybe 'involving' would be better than 'having'; but I doubt the rendering altogether. The phrase is quite unique in N.T. Scriptures. I believe that λόγος means 'talk.' Twice the Apostle uses the term in a depreciatory sense, in 1 Cor. iv. 19, and in 1 Thess. i. 5. In both places λόγος, 'mere talk,' is opposed to δύναμις, 'effective power.' What he seems to be here implying is that such prohibitions carry with them a seeming reasonableness. When you hear them you say, How wise! What a very excellent counsel! Experience, however, proves that it never goes further than λόγος. There is really nothing in it. Rigorous austerities attract; they seem likely to achieve what their professors claim for them. As a matter of fact, they do not. Λόγον ἔχουσι σοφίας ἀλλ' οὐ τὴν δύναμιν. They sound like wisdom, but wisdom they are not. Ἐθελοθρησκεία appears to be a Pauline coinage. In LXX there are no such words. But Plato has ἐθελοδουλεία (for 'willing slavery'); Polybius ἐθελοκάκησις (for 'wilful neglect of duty'); Thucydides has ἐθελοπρόξενος (for 'one who takes on himself the duty of *proxenos*'). Ἐθελόσοφος (for 'would be wise') and ἐθελοφιλόσοφος ('would be philosopher') are found in later writers. The oldest of them all is ἐθελόκωφος ('pretending deafness'). No doubt some idea of pretence or unreality attaches to the Apostle's word. An ἐθελοθρῆσκος is one who undertakes religious observances beyond the common, and that too of his own initiative. Maybe the ἐθελο should be carried on to the ταπεινοφροσύνῃ, so that the whole expression would imply 'self-imposed austerities and *self-chosen* humiliations.' Compare the προπαθόντες καὶ (προ)ὑβρισθέντες of 1 Thess. ii. 2. Ἀφειδεία σώματος would apply (so L.) to the hardships of the soldier, the toils of the earnest student, or the rigours of the ascetic. St. Paul (be it remembered) 'led' his own body 'a sad life' (1 Cor. ix. 27), but in the way of unsparing usage, like the Athenians of Thucydides, not in the way of self-imposed discipline.

There is in L. an excellent citation from Philo, describing the austere life of the Therapeutes in Egypt (a body of Judaic mystics), which it might be well to render: 'They feast luxuriously on wisdom (σοφίας), which supplies them richly and bountifully with new *tenets* (δόγματα). Only at intervals of six days do they taste of the barest food. Their bread is cheap, their only relish salt. Their drink is spring water. *Satiety* of soul and body (πλησμονὴν . . . ψυχῆς καὶ σώματος) they avoid as an evil and dangerous thing.' It will be noted that the two terms common to St. Paul and Philo are not used in the same senses. St. Paul's δόγματα are 'rules,' not 'doctrines'; his πλησμονή is not 'satiety' but the 'endeavour to satisfy,' or rather 'indulgence.'

The last few words of the chapter are notoriously puzzling. 'This Epistle as a whole' (says Dr.

Hort) 'and more especially its second Chapter appears to have been ill preserved in ancient times; and it may be that some of the hardnesses . . . are really due to primitive corruption.' Verses 18 and 23 were no doubt in the writer's mind. In *v.* 23 there most plainly should be a developed antithesis. As the text now stands, it is not very obvious. The ascetic practices of which mention is made are apparently 'wise'—wise because they use the body hardly, and that (one might suppose) is good for the spiritual life, as subduing the *σάρξ* or 'animal nature.' If we still possess what the Apostle wrote in the letter's original, this antithesis must reside in the closing words of all; that is, in *οὐκ ἐν τιμῇ τινὶ πρὸς πλησμονὴν τῆς σαρκός*. If it be so, it must be confessed that *πλησμονή* is strangely used and the preposition still more strangely. For *πλησμονή* must mean 'pampering,' whereas it should mean 'repletion'; and *πρός* must mean 'against,' whereas it should mean 'in regard to.' Still, render it any other way and all sense disappears. What is one to make of the English of our fathers, "Which things have indeed show of wisdom *in willworship* and humility and *neglecting of the body*; not in any honour to the *satisfying of the flesh*"? All one can say of that is, that it means precisely nothing. I have wondered whether possibly we might substitute for *πλησμονήν* such a word as *ἐπιλησμοσύνην*, "not of any value in regard to forgetting the flesh."

Unless I am wholly mistaken, I believe that those who have tried the way of asceticism would admit it does not bring that sense of self-mastery which its votaries desiderate. And this appears to be what the Apostolic writer is saying. But it is not as plainly stated in the text that has come down to us as we could wish to have it.

However, it should be said that the antithesis required may not be given at all (as Winer argues). In that case *οὐκ ἐν τιμῇ τινί* might, with reasonable probability, be taken as applying to the body which 'is held in no account.' *Πρὸς πλησμονὴν τῆς σαρκός* would remain a perplexity. It then would have to afford us the ground for the body's disregard. Could we make anything of this: 'not held of any account in view of fleshly satiety'? That might conceivably mean that the body was nothing regarded because its consistent indulgence brought nothing but the sense of surfeit. But (once again) I doubt.

## CHAPTER III

THE readers are now called upon no longer to regard the old dead past. They 'died with Christ' in Baptism, and that implied death to 'the world' and all that is merely material. For as they mystically shared His death, so did they also His uprising. Resurrection as well as death is symbolised in the Font. And the key which unlocks the gate to this new and risen life we were told in ii. 12 is 'faith.'

If, then, the great change has come and 'death' has been indeed the passage to a new 'life,' let them live accordingly and once for all discard what belongs to a lower plane!

iii. 1-4. "If, I say, you were raised with Christ set your hearts on the realm above, *where Christ is,* seated high at God's right hand. Breathe the atmosphere of heaven and not of earth. For die you did, and your life is hidden away *with Christ* '*in God.*' When Christ, our Life, shall be revealed, then shall you also be manifested with Him in glory."

It matters not whether one says 'if you have been raised' or 'if you were raised.' All that is needful is that we should employ an English past tense. "*If ye be risen*" is incorrect, though doctrinal difference there happens to be none: it is merely a question of accurate and precise grammatical expression. On the other hand, it should be admitted, St. Paul apparently shrinks from using the perfect passive of this verb about 'believers.' Christ "*is raised*" (ἐγήγερται), but twice over in 1 Cor. xv. the writer definitely shuns the employment of the same tense in the case of still living Christians. Their 'raising' is not consummated yet. It will not be till the end. Maybe this is the explanation of his usage, which is certainly a fact. For the 'mystical' joint-dying and joint-rising the aorist is a very proper tense. The perfect hardly would be.

Our 'rising with Christ,' once more, did not come when He was raised, but when we by incorporation became sharers in His death and in His life.

"*The things above*" (τὰ ἄνω) is a phrase found only here—in this chapter, that is—in Pauline scripture. In the Gospel of St. John we find it again, "*I am from the world above*," ἐγὼ ἐκ τῶν ἄνω εἰμί (St. John viii. 23). That τὰ ἄνω (so to speak) describes a *place* is made clear by the following "*where*." Ambitions, thoughts and hopes, all must turn to heaven. Where Christ is, there the believer's heart should ever be. "*Seated on the right hand of God*" recalls the prophetic utterance of Psalm cx. i. Possibly this fact helps to strengthen the contention of L. that the "*is*" must be separated from the "*seated.*" The phrase rendered in our familiar A.V. "*set your affections on things above*" is reminiscent of the well-known saying of Christ in the Gospel story, addressed to the tempter Peter, "*Thou savourest not the things that be of God, but the things that be of men*" (a decidedly better rendering than the Revisers' substitute), *οὐ φρονεῖς τὰ τοῦ Θεοῦ ἀλλὰ τὰ τῶν ἀνθρώπων.* A broad and free translation is essential to represent it. Similar usages are found in Rom. viii. 5, "*for they that are after the flesh do mind the things of the flesh*" (φρονοῦσι τὰ τῆς σαρκός), and Phil. iii. 19, *οἱ τὰ ἐπίγεια φρονοῦντες* ("*people that are of earthly mind*").

The φρονεῖν plainly expresses the whole mood of the man, his whole outlook upon things.

The words that follow repeat the doctrine of Philippians, but in a more impressive form. See Phil. iii. 20, 21.

> "For our *citizenship* (πολίτευμα) *is in heaven*
> wherefrom also" (that is, from our πολίτευμα)
> "*we expect* a Saviour
> the Lord Jesus Christ,
> Who shall fashion anew
> the body of our humiliation
> that it may be conformable
> to the body of His Glory
> according to His wonder-working ability
> (κατὰ τὴν ἐνέργειαν τοῦ δύνασθαι αὐτόν)
> to subdue all things to Himself."

Compare this with the statement of the text that lies before us.

The "*citizenship in heaven*" answers to the "*heaven above, where Christ is*"; Christ's *manifestation*" here corresponds to the "*looking for a Saviour*" there; our own "*manifestation in glory*," as promised in Colossians, reproduces the Philippian teaching as to the wondrous transformation Christ's power will produce in us. Only, here the supreme result is not attributed immediately to Him. Yet (as L. so well reminds us) it is "Christ," "Christ," "Christ," "Christ," four times over, and He is most emphatically declared to be our 'Life.' On the other hand, the impressive conception of the present concealment of the thing which belongs to us and its future manifestation is here present, absent there.

Notice the characteristic touch by which it is "*your life*" in *v.* 3 and "*our Life*" in *v.* 4. When the 'life' of the Christian man is identified with Christ Himself (compare the famous dictum in St. John) St. Paul will not be left out. THE LIFE belongs to all. For the concluding "*You shall be manifested with Him*" one necessarily compares 1 John iii. 2: for the "*in glory*" Rom. viii. 17 and St. John xvii. 22 supply apt parallels.

In Ephesians ii. this great consummation is spoken of as potentially achieved. There it runs:

> "God . . . hath quickened us
> together with Christ
> (συνεζωοποίησεν τῷ Χριστῷ)
> and raised us up with Him
> and made us to sit with Him
> in the heavenly places
> (συνεκάθισεν ἐν τοῖς ἐπουρανίοις) . . ."

to which statement is attached (lest we forget!) the reminder

"in Christ Jesus" (Ephes. ii. 5, 6),

recalling that He is 'Saviour' and 'Life,' as He is here. Κέκρυπται, of course, expresses that our 'life' is truly there, although the world cannot see it, nor indeed can we ourselves entirely realise it.

The verb "*manifest*" (φανεροῦν) is mainly used of the historic manifestation of the Lord Jesus on an earthly stage. Here only is it applied to the manifestation which is not yet.

"In God" (ἐν τῷ Θεῷ) is a phrase which seems to call for comment. L. does not speak of it. The aptest illustration I can think of is in the 'High Priestly Prayer,' St. John xvii. 22, 23. It is a good deal more (is it not?) than the Philippian "*in the heavenlies.*" But it is just the sort of phrase one dares not speak about. Our 'life' is hidden, and Christ Himself is 'hidden'; but He is with the Father, and our 'life' (though unrealised yet) is safe in the Father's keeping.

The ὅταν marks the time of Christ's manifestation (and ours) as uncertain in its incidence. In 1 John iii. the thing is expressed with a considerably ampler vagueness: there it says ἐὰν φανερωθῇ (1 John iii. 2). And yet there are always people who tell us exactly when it is going to happen. What do they do with their minds when they study Holy Scripture?

This sublime conception of the "*life hidden with Christ in God*" is the Apostle's remedy for all moral frailty. It is not ascetic rigour which will master fleshly temptation. It is the 'expulsive power' of a new and grand idea which will best achieve it. Our Lord had said, when on earth, "*Where thy treasure is, there will thy heart be.*" This principle plainly applies to the Christian man. If his 'heart' is where his very 'life' is, then plainly his fleshly impulses will have little chance indeed to drag him down. But thereto an effort is needed, an effort to be inspired by the splendour of the great truth.

The admonition which follows begins with a cryptic utterance, "*Kill then your members which are upon the earth.*" The verb for 'kill,' 'make dead,' is a word unknown to the Classics, unknown even in the LXX. But we have it in an epitaph on a Greek of the 'Roman' period, 'Man, pass not by my poor dead body' (σῶμά μου τὸ νενεκρωμένον); and Plutarch employs the same term to describe the frozen condition of that body from which heat has fled: he calls it νεκρωθεῖσαν ('made dead'). That the verb, at the time of writing, was common in daily use is proved by this, that St. Paul and the writer of Hebrews both employ its perfect passive participle to describe the condition of Abraham at the time when he believed God's promise of a son. Apart from those two usages the verb is found only here. In 2 Cor. iv. 10 we have the very difficult expression "*always bearing about in our body the dying* (νέκρωσιν) *of Jesus.*" The exhortation to 'slay,' to 'do to death,' is intelligible enough. But what are we to do to death? It says "*our members on the earth.*" I believe it to be a fact that, when St. Paul wishes to speak of the 'body,' the mortal 'body,' as a seat and a source of 'sin,' he prefers not to call it 'body' (σῶμα), but rather μέλη ('limbs'). This applies especially to Romans (see chapters vi. and vii.). We must always bear in mind that the "animal body" of earth (the σῶμα ψυχικόν) is regarded by St. Paul as the "seed" of the "spiritual body," the σῶμα πνευματικόν.

"*Kill then your earthly body,*" he says. The extreme vigour of this saying is best exemplified by the very 'watery' sense which in the course of years has attached to 'mortify.' *Mortificate membra vestra* says the Vulgate, and (for all I know to the contrary) the old Latin may have said the same. That is a very suitable rendering for the verb which the Greek presents. But "*mortify*" isn't at all. It suggests to the modern reader exactly and precisely what St. Paul is deprecating, that is, a disciplinary rigour which will tame the 'fleshly' passions. So true is it of error that it is like the hydra's head! The body is to be "killed" by resolute remembrance of higher things. The "*old man*" in us is dead: then let it be dead! Don't wake it to new life! "*Live in the spirit,*" as he says elsewhere (Gal. v. 16), "*and ye shall never fulfil the desire of the flesh*" (καὶ ἐπιθυμίαν σαρκὸς οὐ μὴ τελέσητε). It is the same thing differently stated. To "*live in* (or by) *the spirit*" is really the same thing as to live the new, the heavenly life, to realise the heavenly 'citizenship.' The mystical 'death,' in fact, must be faithfully followed out by the Christian while living on earth. If he is 'dead' to earthly things, he *is* 'dead' to earthly things. Let him live accordingly. *Cor in coelo* must be his motto.

I feel sure that the right understanding of this passage requires that we should not take the catalogue of the vices which follows as though they were the 'members.' Of course they are not. That is to say, from *νεκρώσατε* (which aptly applies to the *μέλη*, but no further) we must supply another verb. It is a normal Pauline 'zeugma.' Unhappily, no rendering will make the 'parable' with which the paragraph opens intelligible to English readers. It is essentially Pauline, but somewhat too forceful for us, with our colder, duller natures.

iii. 5, 6. "Kill then your earthly bodies! Fornication, uncleanness, sodomy (?), lewd desire,—(away with them all!) and greed, for it is idolatry; for which things' sake doth come the wrath of God."

Most editors omit "*on the children of disobedience*," which seems to have made its way into the later texts from Ephes. v. 6.

The parallel in Ephesians should be closely considered.

"But fornication and all uncleanness or overreaching (*πλεονεξία*) let it not even be named among you, as becometh folks that are 'holy' (*καθὼς πρέπει ἁγίοις*)! And (let there be no) filthiness and foolish talking or jesting, which should not be at all (*ἃ οὐκ ἀνῆκεν*), but rather giving of thanks. For this you can easily see (*τοῦτο γὰρ ἴστε γιγνώσκοντες*), that any fornicator or

unclean person or overreacher (which is an idolater) has no inheritance in the kingdom of Christ and God."
(Ephes. v. 3-5.)

The word "overreaching" (πλεονεξία) in this passage from Ephesians looks as though it ought to represent some distinctly fleshly sin. The words "*let it not even be named*" seem to me to point that way. It is well known that in 1 Thess. iv. 6 the curious word "overreach" is definitely used in connexion with adultery. The words are, "*that no one outstep and overreach his brother in the matter*," and the context makes it plain that the special form of wrongful advantage taken over the ill-used brother is in relation to the marriage tie. Moreover, in 1 Cor. v. 10, 11 the noun πλεονέκτης is used in so close connexion with πόρνος that it seems a fair inference that it may bear some such significance. I am not claiming that it does in Colossians, but I think it does in Ephesians. Of course I recognise that in both Epistles πλεονεξία is identified with 'idolatry.' It is possible that in Ephes. v. 5 πλεονέκτης bears a different sense from the πλεονεξία that comes two verses before it. The four terms which have to do with the bodily passions do not (I should say) exhibit an accurate classification. They are rather four instances of sins of the kind. Πορνεία I render 'fornication,' but it seems to cover more in N.T. usage. Ἀκαθαρσία is, it would seem, a more general term. In Latin *pathicus* has a definite sense; perhaps πάθος refers to that vice. Ἐπιθυμία κακή (maybe) covers sins of incest.

The 'worship of the golden calf' in all its myriad forms, the lust of mere possession, we can easily understand as being classed with idolatry. Our Lord said Himself "*You cannot serve God and mammon*," and L. quotes from Philo and others passages that illustrate this special identification.

The present ἔρχεται ("*comes*") expresses the eternal truth which man is ever forgetting, There is a God and He does 'hate' these things. On the other hand, to be sure, it may mean "*is coming*" and be virtually a future. If the verb be a virtual future the "*Wrath*" becomes technical, as in St. John.

One further statement is made about these heathen vices before we pass on to another passionate appeal to have done with the bad old life.

iii. 7. "Wherein you too once walked, when your life was among them."

In Ephes. ii. 3 we find a somewhat similar relative clause where the relative must be masculine. Here it is neuter. The neuter in such expressions (L. points out) is more usual. With περιπατεῖν ἐν, it may be said, a 'thing' or 'things' is invariable, except with ἐν αὐτῷ ("*in Him*") where, of course, the ἐν αὐτῷ is not so closely associated with the verb. (In Ephes. *l.c.* the verb is a different one, *ἀνεστράφημεν.*) I believe ἐζῆτε ἐν τούτοις means what the paraphrase implies, that these things in old days very largely constituted their life. Many people still count them as being of the very essence of it.

In the old days (I repeat) they were devoted to these things; but there is a 'now' opposed to that 'then.'

iii. 8-10. "But *now* put you too away from yourselves *every bit of it*! anger, passion, malice, slander, vile talk upon your lips. Lie not to one another. Do off the old man with his doings and do on the new, that evermore is *freshened* in growing knowledge, after the pattern of Him that made him."

There can be no question that we have here, at the end of the paragraph, a double reference to Genesis; to the creative word in chapter i. "*Let us make man after our image and likeness*" (*ποιήσωμεν ἄνθρωπον κατ' εἰκόνα ἡμετέραν καὶ καθ' ὁμοίωσιν*), Gen. i. 26; and (I think) also to Gen. iii. 22, "*And God said, Lo! Adam is become as one of us, for to know good and evil*" (*τοῦ γιγνώσκειν καλὸν καὶ πονηρόν*). *Now*, under the new Creation, the acquisition of knowledge is open to all. Deeper and deeper into wisdom the believer may daily probe. There is no limit to this growth, where the Holy Spirit is.

But before the 'new man' can be 'put on'—that is, the regenerate life in all its fulness—every one of the old bad ways must be put aside. Other Christians have done it; so must the Colossians. Τὰ *πάντα* means "*all of it*," every element that goes to make up the heathen life. A number of them are mentioned: 'wrath' (*ὀργή*) which is lasting, and 'passion' (*θυμός*) which is explosive; 'malice' (*κακία*), the temper which makes a man want to do wrong, the source and fountain-head of injustice and of cruelty and of every hurtful usage of our neighbour; 'slander' (*βλασφημία*), a vice exceedingly characteristic of the man who loves not God; 'vile speaking' (*αἰσχρολογία*), a term of twofold significance, for it applies both to unseemly talk and also to abusive. It is unmistakably used by Xenophon in the former sense, by Polybius in the latter. But they are closely akin, for the abusive man (we all know) is generally foul-mouthed too. In Ephes. v. instead of *αἰσχρολογία* we have *αἰσχρότης*, which plainly applies to foul talk, and that is probably the predominant sense in this passage.

"*Lie not to one another*," he says. A reference to Ephes. iv. 25 (where 'lying' comes first in the catalogue of evil things to be put away) suggests that the addition of 'to one another' is by no means otiose.

"Wherefore putting away" (ἀποθέμενοι, as ἀπόθεσθε in v. 8) "the lie, speak truth, each man with his neighbour, for we are *members of one another* (ὅτι ἐσμὲν ἀλλήλων μέλη)."

Falsehood violates brotherhood. It also is an offence in other directions, but with them at the moment the writer has no concern.

In St. Paul *παλαιός* always bears a depreciatory sense. We have "*the old leaven*" in 1 Corinthians, "*the old*" (that is, obsolete) "*Covenant*" in 2 Corinthians, and "*the old man*" in Rom. vi. 6 (where it stands for the "*old self*," that was crucified with Christ, that it might make way for the new), in Ephes. iv., and here.

The usage in Ephesians and Colossians is not the same as in Romans. There it is "*our* old man"—as I have already explained equivalent to "our old self;" here it is "*the old man*," "*the new man*"—a different matter. The expression indeed is strange. But there is no help for it. It must represent what we should express by the 'old *manhood*,' the 'new *manhood*.' It is put, perhaps, in a concrete form, partly because so is the Apostle's way; partly because we are not concerned with the speculative abstract, but with the practical, personal concrete, every one of us. Ephesians says:

"So surely as . . . you were taught, . . . that *you* should put away the old man" (κατὰ τὴν προτέραν ἀναστροφήν seems to be misplaced: it would naturally be a phrase qualifying τὸν παλαιὸν ἄνθρωπον: where it is, it makes little sense) "that is passing on to ruin because it follows delusive lusts, and be renewed (ἀνανεοῦσθαι) in the spirit of your understanding; aye, put on (ἐνδύσασθαι) the new man (καινὸν ἄνθρωπον) that after God has been created" (it is the new creation, I feel certain, that is referred to, not the old) "in righteousness and holy sincerity" (if that be the meaning of the last very difficult clause).

(Ephes. iv. 21-24.)

The resemblance at once and the divergence are very noteworthy. In both we have the 'putting on' expressed in the *aorist* tense, for the ἐνδυσάμενοι carries with it (I feel sure) the 'momentary' sense of the ἐνδύσασθαι; in both we have the "*old man*"; in both we have, though in very different phraseology, a mention of creation "*after*"

God or the "*likeness of God*"; in both also there is mention of a continuous process of renewal. So much for the resemblances. As for differences: the "*new man*" is the *καινὸς ἄνθρωπος* in the one, the *νεὸς ἄνθρωπος* in the other; while "*to be renewed*" is in the one *ἀνανεοῦσθαι,* in the other *ἀνακαινοῦσθαι.* Ephesians has *ἀνανεοῦσθαι* and *καινὸς ἄνθρωπος*; Colossians *νεὸς* (*ἄνθρωπος*) and *ἀνακαινούμενον.* What conclusion forces itself upon the plain man while he contemplates these phenomena? Plainly that it is no use suggesting that there is any distinction to be drawn between *νεός* and *καινός* in significance. *Νεός* ought to be 'young' (that is, new in relation to itself), and *καινός* 'fresh' (new in relation to other things), but no such distinction will hold. The meaning of *νεός* and *καινός* is determined by the antithesis with *παλαιός*; and similarly the two verbs, for all their apparent difference, mean precisely the same, simply "*be made new.*"

The paraphrase gives what I consider to be the force of *εἰς ἐπίγνωσιν.* That too has a sort of parallel in the "*be renewed in the spirit of your understanding*" (*ἀνανεοῦσθαι τῷ πνεύματι τοῦ νοὸς ὑμῶν*). The spiritualisation of the *νοῦς* there balances with the "*growth in* (spiritual) *knowledge*" here. In both it is a process indefinitely continued; that is, as long as life lasts. *Τοῦ κτίσαντος* (as L. maintains) is probably God the Father. The undoubted reference to Genesis demands this. Yet it is the 'new' creation which is contemplated in both Epistles.

The thought of the splendour of the new manhood and of the new creation interrupts the train of practical counsels for a moment. The Apostle is overpowered for a while by the sense of that astounding oneness which stamps and characterises the grandeur of the new order.

L. (I think) is wrong in saying that the 'new man' to be 'put on' is not Christ Himself. For He is identical with the "*new Man*" for all purposes. This is shown by the parallel in Galatians to the verse which follows here. For Galatians says:

"All of you that have been baptised into Christ did put on Christ." (Gal. iii. 27.)

It passes on *οὐκ ἐνὶ* Ἰουδαῖος οὐδ' Ἕλλην ("there *can be* neither Jew nor Greek" R.V.). Observe it does not say where this impossibility of divergence exists, but it is obviously in "*Christ.*" So must it be with our "*where*" (ὅπου). It is in the "*New Man*"—in "*Christ*"—that all these differences and distinctions vanish. All are lost, obliterated in one prodigious union.

iii. 11. "*There* can there be no 'Jew and Gentile,' 'circumcision and uncircumcision,' barbarian, Scythian, slave, freeman; but CHRIST is ALL and everywhere."

'Jew and Gentile' should be printed so because it is a normal pair, as is 'circumcision and uncircumcision.' The latter terms may be employed in their 'gregarious' sense, 'circumcision' meaning 'circumcised people'; but it is not necessary to take it so. A 'barbarian' would naturally be opposed to a 'Greek'; but he cannot be here, for 'Greek' has already done duty for 'Gentile.' A *barbaros* is one who 'jabbers,' that is, speaks with undue swiftness an unintelligible tongue. The ancient use of the term (with its wider late connotation) was the flat denial of the brotherhood of man. As for the word itself, it comes but four times in the New Testament. It is found in the 'Classical' antithesis ('Greek' and 'non-Greek') in Rom. i. 14; in 1 Cor. xiv. 11 for one 'speaking gibberish'; and in Acts xxviii. twice over, for the 'natives' of Melita. Broadly speaking, it is out of place in a Christian atmosphere. Christ has made an end of it as a term of contempt. The 'Scythians' were regarded as the lowest of all 'barbarians.' 'Bond and free' are not coupled as in Galatians, nor have we in Colossians mention of the abolition of the fundamental distinction of all distinctions, the great division of sex. Here all terms are poured out at the end pell-mell, in one great stream, "barbarian, Scythian, bond, free." We break away from all order and classification, and hurry on to the great pronouncement that closes the whole matter, "but *CHRIST* is ALL and in all."

The τὰ πάντα must be noted. In no conceivable form could the thing be more strongly expressed. He is coincident with the whole of the New Manhood. *Where that is, He is.* Ἐν πᾶσιν (as I think) is better taken as an adverbial expression of place. So should I take it, for instance, in 1 Cor. xii. 6 (ὁ αὐτὸς Θεὸς ὁ ἐνεργῶν τὰ πάντα ἐν πᾶσιν, "*Who produces all effects, wherever they are*").

We now return to the conception of 'putting on,' not now indeed the 'putting on' of the New Manhood or the 'putting on' of Christ, but the 'donning' of those qualities which are essentially *His* qualities.

iii. 12. "Put on then as the great God's chosen ones, holy, beloved . . ."

Ἐκλεκτός is fairly common with the genitive Θεοῦ or τοῦ Θεοῦ. It is used of Christ Himself in two places of the Gospel (St. Luke xxiii. 35, St. John i. 34; not Tisch. or W. H. in the latter passage). The genitive is probably 'possessive.' "*God's Elect*" occurs in St. Paul in Rom. viii. 33 and Titus i. 1. One might be tempted to regard it as meaning 'persons chosen of (that is, by) God' (compare the use of διδακτοί in St. John vi. 45 and 1 Cor. ii. 13); but I do not think it will do. In any case ἐκλεκτοί, ἅγιοι and ἠγαπημένοι are all terms which belong to the new Israel of right. The old Israel aforetime had been so denominated. 'Holy' (of course) implies consecration, not moral blamelessness. The 'holiness' of the Old Covenant was entirely secured by outward rites.

But let us see what things these highly favoured ones, God's people, must put on.

iii. 12-15. "Put on then as the great God's chosen ones, holy, beloved, a tender, compassionate heart, lowliness, gentleness, patience under affront; bearing with one another and forgiving one another, if any have a complaint against any. As the Lord has forgiven you, even so do you (forgive). To crown all put on love. That is the main tie of perfectness. And let the peace of God rule in your hearts, whereunto ye were called, one body all of you. Moreover, be thankful."

It is plain that *σπλάγχνα* by itself bears the sense of 'tenderness': consider Phil. i. 8, and still more Phil. ii. 1 (*εἴ τις σπλάγχνα καὶ οἰκτιρμοί*). Hence the rather cumbrous paraphrase. *Χρηστότης* is 'kindness' in the broadest sense. God Himself is called *χρηστός* in the Gospel even by the Lord Jesus Christ (St. Luke vi. 35). St. Paul too talks of the "*kindness*" of God in Rom. ii. 4, where our English renders "*goodness.*" We often, of course, use 'good' instead of 'kind' in the daily speech.

*Ταπεινοφροσύνη* is not a 'classical' word, nor is it in LXX. In late Greek it bears an ill sense, except in Christian writings. Josephus, for instance, says the Emperor Galba was murdered in mid forum *αἰτιαθεὶς ἐπὶ ταπεινοφροσύνῃ*; but what they meant by it I can't be sure. Was it 'cowardice' or 'meanness'? Tacitus would seem to suggest the latter. *Ταπεινόφρων* is used by Plutarch for 'mean-spirited.' Christ startled His own followers by claiming Himself to be 'lowly,' *ταπεινός* (St. Matthew xi. 29). From that time forward 'lowliness' ranked among Christians as a virtue. Yet even in St. Paul the adjective *ταπεινός* is found in its ancient heathen sense of 'mean' not 'humble' (see 2 Cor. x. 1). 'Humility' in Philippians is the state of mind which ranks one's neighbour above oneself (Phil. ii. 3). That is much the same sense it has here. A man is *πραΰς* (says L.) who is not rough or rude; 'gentle' is what we call it now, rather than 'meek.' *Μακροθυμία*, which we have met already in chapter i. 11, means originally 'long temper'—a word we unhappily have not, though we have its opposite—and so 'forbearance.' It is an attribute of God, in regard to offending man, in many places. The participial phrases of *v.* 13 illustrate mainly the last of these virtues: *ἀνέχεσθαι* means to 'put up with,' used chiefly with persons for object, but not invariably. *Χαρίζεσθαι* in the sense 'forgive' is a Lucano-Pauline term. It comes first in the famous parable of the Two Debtors, "*he frankly forgave them both,*" *ἀμφοτέροις ἐχαρίσατο* (St. Luke vii. 42). Apart from this one Gospel instance, it only means 'forgive' in 2 Corinthians, Ephesians and Colossians. Whatever distinction may be drawn between the two 'reciprocals' *ἀλλήλους* and *ἑαυτούς* in other places, I very much doubt whether any can be drawn here and in Ephesians. Ephes. iv. 32 says:

> "Be ye kind to one another (*εἰς ἀλλήλους*), forgiving one another (*χαριζόμενοι ἑαυτοῖς*), as God in Christ has forgiven you."

It is over-subtle, I think, to say that the latter 'reciprocal' emphasises the idea of 'corporate unity.' *Ἐάν τις πρός τινα*, to my mind, seems to regard me and my neighbour as separate individuals, not as members of one body. Therefore I should boldly aver they are used without distinction, for the sake of variety. Notwithstanding, L.'s instances from Xenophon are highly interesting.

The concrete *μομφή* ('quarrel,' *querela*, that is, 'ground of complaint') seems to be one of that large class of words which belong to the poets and to common speech. It is not an accepted 'Prose' term. The impressive appeal to forgive is a separate sentence. The double καί ('also') is Greek; but it is not English. "*The Lord*" may be (as L. suggests) a link with Our Master's parable. Maybe we should render "*your Lord*": that would emphasise the idea of owed allegiance (cf. iv. 1). Verse 14 tells us that 'love' is to be the crown and coping-stone of Christian character. Its relation to all virtue is set forth in a singular phrase: "*which thing* (ὅ) *is the 'bond' of perfectness.*" Σύνδεσμος might mean 'bundle'; but here it certainly does not. In Acts we have it for 'fetter' (viii. 23); in Ephesians we have the expression, "*to maintain the oneness of the spirit in* (by means of ?) *the bond of peace*" (τηρεῖν τὴν ἑνότητα τοῦ πνεύματος ἐν τῷ συνδέσμῳ τῆς εἰρήνης, Ephes. iv. 3). We had it in ii. 19, in a surgical figure. Here it means that which ties, or keeps together. Love is the main tie or bond of τελειότης ('perfectness'). 'Perfectness' I would associate with the famous saying of Christ, "*Ye shall be therefore perfect*" (St. Matthew v. 43).

In Phil. iv. 7 "*the Peace of God,*" we are told, "*shall be sentry over our hearts,*" 'shall guard them as an armed guard' (φρουρήσει). Here it is not to be 'guard' but 'ruler.' L.'s own instances plainly demonstrate that there is no idea of 'umpire" in the verb βραβευέτω. When he quotes Polybius as saying, 'Everything the Galatians do is *governed* rather by impulse than by reason' (βραβεύεται θυμῷ μᾶλλον ἢ λογισμῷ), and Philo as declaring that 'the fool flings away reason, the charioteer and βραβεύτης (of the soul),' I conceive he makes it plain that βραβεύειν only means 'govern.' Probably also μηδεὶς ὑμᾶς καταβραβευέτω, in ii. 18, means only "*Let no one overmaster you*" or "*overrule you*," that is, 'crush you with his authority.' Βραβεύειν probably has lost all its figurative sense. There is no 'umpiring' at all about it! But others may think otherwise. Εἰς ἣν καὶ ἐκλήθητε ἐν ἑνὶ σώματι ("*to which you were called in one body*"), I believe, means 'to which you were called *to be realised in one body.*' The phrase ἐν ἑνὶ σώματι defies grammatical analysis. Of course the ἐν ἑνὶ σώματι might be virtually equivalent to ἓν σῶμα ὄντες. The "*one body and one spirit*" of Ephes. iv., I think, may best be taken as a phrase in apposition with the subject of ἐκλήθητε:

> "I beseech you therefore to walk worthily of the calling wherewith you were called . . . endeavouring to maintain . . . as one body with one spirit."
>
> (Ephes. iv. 1-3.)

Yet directly after we have (in Ephesians) "as ye were called *with* one hope of your calling," ἐν μιᾷ ἐλπίδι τῆς κλήσεως—an instrumental comitative, one would say. We might accordingly represent our phrase by this, "*with one body*," or the like. But it is difficult to say. It is of interest to note the various aims and ends with which in Pauline writings the expression 'ye were called' is linked. In 1 Cor. i. 9 it is "*into fellowship in His Son*" (εἰς κοινωνίαν τοῦ υἱοῦ αὐτοῦ); in Gal. v. 13 it is "*to be free*" (ἐπ' ἐλευθερίᾳ); in 1 Tim. vi. 12 to "*eternal life*." There is no phrase quite like this in regard to form. The grace of 'thankfulness' concludes the paragraph. That can never be left out by one who knows. Christian worship clearly centres in *Eucharistia*. The adjective is only here.

We pass on to discourse about utterance. How shall a Christian man employ his power of speech? Hear the Apostolic answer.

It is not wholly plain; for it opens with an unexampled phrase, and six words further on comes a clause of doubtful attachment. "*Let the 'word of Christ' dwell in you richly*," it begins. What is meant by "the word of Christ"? "The Word of God" or "the Word" is a common N.T. phrase for what we call 'the Gospel.' But this is plainly different. Is it like the Johannine formulæ referred to by Bishop Lightfoot, such as 1 John ii. 14, "because ye are strong and *God's word abides in you*"? I should doubt it. "Christ's word" must either mean (I should say) 'the way Christ speaks' or 'speech about Christ.' Their lips are to be full of Christ, and so are their hearts. For λόγος covers 'thought' as well as 'word.' And this λόγος, though it find expression in Psalms and Hymns, is to have its seat in the heart. 'Ενοικείτω ("Let it dwell in you") would indicate that.

Next, how are we to marshal the words "*in all wisdom*"? They may belong to what goes before or to what follows after. The σοφία, I should hold, is Christian σοφία, a full and adequate grasp of the wonder of God's love. It is the kind of σοφία of which we read in 1 Cor. ii. 6. The sense seems to me to be "Let the *thought* of Christ dwell in your hearts *with perfect understanding.*" May Christ occupy your thoughts and may you understand Him! To the end that it may be so, each must help his brother. Instruction and admonition are very essential. By a common Pauline usage the exhortation to employ these means is conveyed by participles. The imperatival force has to be supplied (that is, drawn) from the preceding imperative. The participle by itself has no such force or value. Let us now proceed to a rendering:

iii. 16, 17. "May Christ and His message dwell in you richly, and may you be altogether wise! Teach one another and admonish one another, by God's good grace, with psalms, with hymns, with spiritual songs; singing in your hearts to God. And anything you do, in word or in deed, let it be all in the Name of the Lord Jesus, with thanksgiving to God the Father through Him."

I do not profess for one moment to be content with this rendering of ὁ λόγος τοῦ Χριστοῦ. I believe it is beyond the power of our language to cope with it. We possess no term at all with all the range of meaning that belongs to the Hellenic λόγος. 'Word,' 'speech,' 'story,' 'message,' 'thought,' 'theory'—none of these is adequate. What the Apostle really prays for then is that they may know all of Christ which is knowable; fully understand all about Him (so far as revelation goes) and be able to explain it. In fact, he has himself gone about to accomplish his own prayers, for he has done all he could to unfold the 'real Christ' before their eyes; not the 'carpenter of Nazareth,' but the πρωτότοκος πάσης κτίσεως (i. 15), the πρωτότοκος ἐκ τῶν νεκρῶν (i. 18), the Head of all Creation and of the Church. 'Wealth' is a favourite metaphor with St. Paul to illustrate God's Mercy, or His Glory, or the wonders of His Grace. Two other verses aptly illustrate the "*richly*" here; Rom. xi. 33, "*O depth of the 'wealth' of the wisdom and knowledge of God,*" where the first καί must either be omitted or regarded not as joining "*wealth*" to "*wisdom,*" but as meaning simply "*both*" (ὦ βάθος πλούτου <καὶ> σοφίας καὶ γνώσεως Θεοῦ), for it is in the "*wisdom*" and "*knowledge*" that the contemplated "*wealth*" consists. They are inconceivably splendid and far-reaching. The other is Ephes. iii. 8, "that I should preach to the Gentiles *the unsearchable wealth of Christ*" (τοῖς ἔθνεσιν εὐαγγελίσασθαι τὸν ἀνεξιχνίαστον πλοῦτον τοῦ Χριστοῦ). It will be seen that the "*wealth of Christ*" in that passage corresponds with the "*word of Christ*" here. It is the whole ineffable revelation of what He is and what He has achieved. (Compare chapter i. 27, and chapter ii. 2.) I don't think ἐν πάσῃ σοφίᾳ means "*in every kind* of wisdom," but "in *all* wisdom." That, I think, is in accord with Pauline usage. A 'Psalm' (ψαλμός) is a sacred song with instrumental accompaniment; for ψάλλειν means to 'twang,' and at once suggests stringed instruments.

A 'Hymn' (ὕμνος) is a song in praise of God. Why, then, it will be asked, is there mention of ᾠδαὶ πνευματικαί, which also can be nothing save 'songs' that are 'religious'? The answer is that probably ὕμνοι are traditional, already established, while the 'spiritual songs' are not.

The same collocation of terms is found in the Ephesian parallel. I will give it all.

"And be not drunk with wine wherein is riot (ἀσωτία), but be filled with the Spirit"; (here is a parallel to the first half of the verse before us) "speaking one to another with psalms and hymns and spiritual songs, singing and making melody (ᾄδοντες καὶ ψάλλοντες) *in your heart* to the Lord, giving thanks always for all to the God and Father, in the Name of Our Lord Jesus Christ, submitting yourselves to one another in the fear of Christ." (Ephes. v. 18-21.)

Here we have the same classification of sacred songs; the same curious addition of the words "*in your hearts*" to 'singing'; the same mention of 'the Name'; the same 'thanksgiving' to God the Father. In our text ἐν τῇ χάριτι belongs, I should say, to the two participles. Why is singing to be "*in your hearts*"? I do not think the Apostle depreciates the music of the lips; he only would have us know that the heart must go with the voice. A 'song' is not a 'song,' unless it be sung; but a hymn to be of any value must be sung with inner reverence.

The subdivision of ποιῆτε ("anything whatever you *do*") into 'word' and 'deed' sounds curious to our ears. The verb for πάντα would be ποιείσθω.

Everything we do or say must be 'auspicated' always with that supremest of Names. Utterance, as such, is not required: one need not *say* 'in the Name,' but the remembrance must never be absent. The participle εὐχαριστοῦντες implies that the spirit of thanksgiving must go with us everywhere, as it went with St. Paul himself. All thanksgiving is offered to God, and it cannot be offered acceptably save "*through Him.*" It is *through Him* we enjoy our sole approach and access to the Throne of Grace. Τῷ Θεῷ πατρί is an unexampled formula. In Ephesians it runs τῷ Θεῷ καὶ πατρί. The absence of the article with Θεῷ would have been more natural.

At this point chapter iii. might very well have ended; for now we plunge into counsels not addressed to the Church as a whole, but addressed to particular classes.

iii. 18–iv. 1. "Wives, submit yourselves to your husbands as belongs to you 'in the Lord.'

Husbands, love your wives and be not ill-tempered towards them.

Children, obey your parents in everything, for this is commendable *for a Christian.*

Fathers, do not *irritate* your children, that they may not lose heart.

Slaves, obey your earthly masters in everything, not with *eyeservice* as '*manpleasers*' but with absolute sincerity, from fear of the One Master. Whatever you are doing, *work at it* with heart and soul, as for the Lord and not for men; being sure that from the Lord you shall receive *the inheritance* as your recompense. It is the Lord Christ Whose slaves you are. The wrong-doer, I say, shall receive the wrong he has done. There is no 'favour' shown.

Masters, afford your slaves justice and fair treatment, being sure that you too have a Master in heaven."

These counsels do not present any special difficulties. They are precepts for the Home (as L. observes). The ἰδίοις of T. R. in *v.* 15 is a late insertion. It would not have needed rendering, had it been read. In late Greek it appears to be far weaker than our 'own.' Wives (I take it) are mentioned first because the home's happiness rests chiefly on this, the maintenance of right relations between the Father and Mother. For practical purposes this (middle or passive) ὑποτάσσεσθαι must be regarded as a deponent. It is better taken so. The ἀνῆκεν is solecistic. It is a mere colloquialism. Were the imperfect used in all strictness (as it would be in the Classics) it would imply that Colossian wives were wholly at fault in this matter. It ought to mean "*as you should have done.*" Ephes. v. 4 presents the same irregularity. L. happily compares our own unscientific use of 'ought' (which clearly should be 'owe'). Where does "*in the Lord*" belong? One may take it with ὑποτάσσεσθε or with ἀνῆκεν. I believe the phrase is equivalent to τοῖς ἐν Κυρίῳ. Therefore I would hold it means in effect "*for Christian people.*" We are living ourselves in times when 'Christian' wives will have to regard themselves as bound by other laws than those who do not claim to be Christ's servants. In the days when the husband's position was more autocratic than it is now (after all our centuries of Christian influence) men no doubt were very apt to lose their tempers at home. The *πικραίνεσθε* here is as the *πικρία* of Ephes. iv. 31. Πικρός properly means 'spiky.' Of things it naturally comes to bear the meaning 'pungent'; of human beings it means 'disagreeable.' The *πικρός* in Aristotle is the man who nurses his anger —in fact, the 'sulky' person. But here it is not quite the same. Observe that the claim of obedience on the child and on the slave is stated in identical terms. Those were, to be sure, the days of *patria potestas.* Yet in the Christian household filial obedience will always rest on a very sure foundation. It is of the very heart of things. In *v.* 20 *εὐαρεστόν* (as L. well says) means "*commendable*"; not here "well-pleasing' to God, as everywhere else, but well-pleasing to all the right-minded. "*In the Lord*" is as above in *v.* 18. It means "*for Christian children.*" The counsel of *v.* 21 is a notable one. Fathers must not 'nag.' They must not always be finding fault on every trivial occasion. That can only have one result. Children soon will give up trying to please people who can't be pleased. Nothing discourages more quickly than parental unreasonableness. It soon begets *ἀθυμία.* Slaves are reminded they have two 'Masters'; a master *κατὰ σάρκα* (which is their peculiar misfortune) and a Master in heaven. 'Master' (remember) connotes ownership. The master of a servant is not a *κύριος*, but a mere employer. The Apostle (as L. bids us mark) knows more about 'slave' feelings from his close and intimate intercourse with the runaway, Onesimus. The striking word "*eyeservice*" (ὀφθαλμοδουλεία), found here and in Ephes. vi. 6, is almost certainly a Pauline coinage. "*Manpleaser,*" on the other hand, is taken from the LXX of Psalm liii. 5. Our Version reads:

"for God hath scattered the bones of him that encampeth against thee."

LXX says, ὁ Θεὸς διεσκόρπισεν ὀστᾶ ἀνθρωπαρέσκων, that is, 'God has scattered abroad the bones of manpleasers.' The term, of course, implies an antithetical 'Godpleaser.' Compare the well-known words of Gal. i. 10, "*Or am I seeking to please men? If at this time of day I were pleasing men, I should not be Christ's servant*" (ἢ ζητῶ ἀνθρώποις ἀρέσκειν; εἰ ἔτι ἀνθρώποις ἤρεσκον Χριστοῦ δοῦλος οὐκ ἂν ἤμην). The fine phrase ἐν ἁπλότητι καρδίας (also in Ephes. vi. 5) is from LXX. It is found there in 1 Chron. xxix. 17, "As for me, in the *uprightness of my heart* I have willingly offered all these things" (LXX ἐν ἁπλότητι καρδίας προεθυμήθην ταῦτα πάντα); and in *Wisdom*, i. 1, "and in *singleness of heart* seek ye Him." We remember what Christ said about undivided allegiance. A slave, of necessity, had to live in a state of fear and apprehension, but (following his Master) St. Paul tells him whom he "ought to fear." (See St. Matthew x. 28.) Only, in this case it is Christ (τὸν Κύριον) Who is to be held in awe. L. justly observes that in ἐργάζεσθε there is an 'advance' on *ποιῆτε.* Ἐκ *ψυχῆς* (' with heart and soul ') is in the Ephesian parallel, but not elsewhere in N.T. The omission of the article with *ἀπὸ Κυρίου* occasions questioning. Where one finds the anarthrous ' Lord,' there is generally a LXX reference. For ' the Lord ' (that is, JEHOVAH) has no article in the Greek O.T. There is no phrase in the ancient scriptures corresponding to what we read here, but (if one may say so) there is about it an O.T. flavour. I should say myself that *ἀπὸ Κυρίου* does not directly refer to Christ, but to what one might call ' God's recompense.' " *Recompense* " (*ἀνταπόδοσις*) is quite a common term in LXX. There is a similar anarthrous phrase in Ephes. vi. 8, in the same connexion. There it is *παρὰ Κυρίου* not *ἀπό*. It makes no real difference. The genitive *τῆς κληρονομίας* is of the ' appositional ' type : the " *inheritance* " forms the recompense.

" *You serve Christ as your Master* " (*τῷ Κυρίῳ Χριστῷ δουλεύετε*) is a parenthetical statement which rather interrupts the tenour of the sentence. This is obvious anyhow, but a reference to Ephes. vi. will make it yet more plain. The *γάρ* of *v.* 25 is due to the break in the sentence. It is of a ' resumptive ' type.

L. has some most instructive remarks on *v.* 25. He reminds us that in Greek eyes a slave was a mere ' chattel ' and could have no rights. We might add, neither could he logically do any wrong (*ἀδικεῖν*). St. Paul readjusts his *status* altogether. He can do wrong : he is a responsible person, as any one else. Ὁ *ἀδικῶν κομίσεται* refers primarily to him. (L. says it refers to both; to slave and to master.) It is most interesting to note that "*wrong*" (ἀδικεῖν) is the very term that the Apostle in the letter to Philemon regards as applicable to Onesimus: "but *if he hath wronged thee* or oweth thee aught, charge it to me" (εἰ δέ τι ἠδίκησέν σε ἢ ὀφείλει, τοῦτο ἐμοὶ ἐλλόγει). The "*if*," of course, in that place does not imply any doubt about it. It is a mere form of speech. "*And there is no respect of persons*" (καὶ οὐκ ἔστιν προσωποληψία): the statement is meant to remove any possible misapprehension in the minds of Christian slaves. If they are dishonest to their earthly masters it will not save them to plead their servile state. As towards Christ and God, they are 'free.' L. quotes Levit. xix. 15, οὐ λήψῃ πρόσωπον πτωχοῦ οὐδὲ μὴ θαυμάσῃς πρόσωπον δυνάστου ("*thou shalt not accept the 'person' of the poor, no, nor shalt thou regard the 'person' of the mighty*"). The judge in Israel is warned that he must hold the balance of justice straight. Neither pity for the poor, nor a desire to please the great must be allowed to deflect the beam. The actual terms προσωποληψία and προσωπολήμπτης are not found in LXX. The expression is only there in its analytical form. In N.T. we have them in Acts x. 34, in Romans ii. 11, in Ephes. vi. 9, and in the Epistle of St. James. Galatians affords an instance of the regular LXX formula πρόσωπον λαμβάνειν (Gal. ii. 6). If slaves are to deal *honestly* by their masters, their masters are to deal *fairly* by them. So says iv. 1. The terms ἴσον and δίκαιον are synonyms in Aristotle. 'Justice' is defined by him (L.) as a 'habit of mind productive of fair dealing, or fairness' (ἕξις ἰσότητος ποιητική). Plainly we must assume that it is much the same with the language here. Τὸ δίκαιον and τὴν ἰσότητα are virtually the same. If a slave does right, he must be given credit for that right: if he does wrong, he must not be treated with undue severity. As long as slaves existed (and St. Paul did not run atilt against existing institutions—as, indeed, why should he?) this was plainly the right and proper way to use and treat them. The great principle that lay at the root of the dealings of a Christian master with a Christian slave is contained in the pronouncement that all believers are Christ's 'slaves.' They are also 'brothers' to one another, and that must, sooner or later, abolish slavery amongst Christian folks. But it has taken long to do it. The old heresy of Aristotle (the φύσει δοῦλος idea) dies hard. And, besides, it has been reinforced by the remembrance of the curse of Ham—a doughty auxiliary, who is also not dead yet.

These counsels for the home reappear, and yet by no means (as a mere copyist would have made them) *totidem verbis*, in Ephesians. The Ephesian form is a good deal the longer. There are three hundred and fourteen words in all, as contrasted with the Colossian one hundred and sixteen. To be sure, the exposition of the 'mystical' aspect of wedlock accounts for a good deal of this. Yet everywhere the wording is longer, in every counsel. What is said to wives here in nine words there takes forty—and even then the principal verb (which, as here, should be ὑποτάσσεσθε) never finds a place for itself, but has to be supplied. For the "as is fitting *in the Lord*" we have the well-known statement about 'headship' which excites so much comment nowadays. The command to husbands to "*love their wives*" is prodigiously expanded in the parallel Epistle. The husband is to the wife as Christ is to the Church. Moreover, husband and wife are 'one' (ἔσονται εἰς σάρκα μίαν, "*shall be one living thing*"), as taught in primitive Genesis. The duty of obedience to parents is there enforced by the citation of the "*first command with promise*" (ἐντολὴ πρώτη ἐν ἐπαγγελίᾳ), a phrase of well-known difficulty. The admonition to fathers is differently expressed. For the ἐρεθίζετε of Colossians we have παροργίζετε. No doubt the effect is the same.

The counsel to slaves and to masters I should like to reproduce here in my own words: the differences are highly interesting. Notable phrases in Ephesians I will italicise:

"Slaves, obey your earthly masters *with fear and trembling* (μετὰ φόβου καὶ τρόμου), in singleness of heart as to Christ; not by the rule of eyeservice (μὴ κατ' ὀφθαλμοδουλείαν) as 'manpleasers,' but as slaves of Christ, *doing the will of God* from the heart (ποιοῦντες τὸ θέλημα τοῦ Θεοῦ), slaving *with good will* (δουλεύοντες μετ' εὐνοίας) as to the Lord and not to men, being sure that *each, if he do any good, shall recover it from the Lord* (κομίσεται παρὰ Κύριου) *be he slave, or be he free.*" (This corresponds, it will be observed, to the statement of 'no favour,' as it comes in Colossians.) "And, masters, deal likewise with them (τὰ αὐτὰ ποιεῖτε πρὸς αὐτούς), *forbearing threatening* (ἀνίεντες τὴν ἀπειλήν), knowing that your own Master too is in heaven; and with Him is no favouritism" (προσωποληψία).

(Ephes. vi. 5-9.)

The two things that strike one most, I should say, as one reads the two sections side by side, are (1) the position of "*with fear and trembling*' (Ephes.) as contrasted with the "*fearing the Lord*" (Col.); and (2) the curious variation in the placing of the statement as to the absence of all 'partiality' with the Heavenly Judge. Yet again, the 'recompense' is attached to ill-doing in the one, to good in the other.

The resemblance seems to point to common authorship; even more so does the divergence. No copyist would have dared to expand the shorter form of Colossians into the longer of Ephesians with such audacity of handling. But one and the same man might very easily say the same things, in much the same words, and yet 'with a difference.' And so he would seem to have done in our two Epistles.

## CHAPTER IV

(FROM *V.* 2)

We pass now to general counsels addressed to all the faithful. These with sundry messages of a personal character complete the text of the letter. They enjoin the duty of prayer, the needfulness of discretion in regard to heathen neighbours and the proper use of speech. They present no special difficulties.

iv. 2-4. "Pray steadily; be wakeful when you pray; be thankful also. Pray too *for me*, that God may open for me a door for the message, that I may tell of the 'mystery' of Christ, which has made me a prisoner; that I may make it plain, as I am bound to tell it."

Precisely the same phrase enjoining constant prayer is found in Rom. xii. 12. In Acts in several places the same verb is similarly used, either with 'prayer' as object (i. 14, vi. 4), or 'teaching' (ii. 42), or the 'ministry of the word' (vi. 4). Sometimes even a person is the object (viii. 13, x. 7). The word exactly corresponds with the

English 'cant' term 'stick to.' *Γρηγορεῖν*, a late formation from the perfect *ἐγρήγορα* (on the analogy of *στήκειν*), means 'to be wide awake,' *vigilare*. In the N.T. *ἀγρυπνεῖν* (which should mean 'to be unable to sleep') is used in just the same sense; so is it too in LXX. *'Αγρυπνεῖν*, indeed, is used in the Ephesian parallel here.

"Praying at every time in spirit, yes, *being wakeful thereunto* (*ἀγρυπνοῦντες εἰς αὐτό*); with all *persistence* (*προσκαρτερήσει*) and supplication for all the saints: *for me too* (*καὶ ὑπὲρ ἐμοῦ*) that *to me may be given utterance* (*δοθῇ λόγος*) in the opening of my lips; that I may freely make known (*ἐν παρρησίᾳ γνωρίσαι*) *the 'Mystery'* of the Gospel, for which *I am an ambassador in a coupling chain* (*ὑπὲρ οὗ πρεσβεύω ἐν ἁλύσει*), that therein *I may speak boldly as I ought to speak* (*ὡς δεῖ με λαλῆσαι*)."
(Ephes. vi. 18-20.)

Once again the same ideas are reproduced with variation of phraseology. Only one idea is absent from Ephesians which is present here. That is 'thanksgiving.' L. is very stout in maintaining that *περὶ ἡμῶν* is a true plural. I believe it is not. The *ὑπὲρ ἐμοῦ* of Ephesians (in connexion with an almost identical petition) would seem to bear me out. The clause *ἵνα . . . ἀνοίξῃ* gives the purport of the prayer: it is a clause of definition. The infinitive *λαλῆσαι*, without an introductory *ὥστε*, is a common type enough in N.T. (cf. Rev. v. 5). The phrase to "*open a door*" recalls 1 Cor. xvi. 9, "*a great door is opened for me and an effectual*" (*θύρα μοι ἀνέῳγεν μεγάλη καὶ ἐνεργής*), and 2 Cor. ii. 12. There is a similar phrase in

Acts xiv. 27. But there the 'door' is 'opened' for the hearers, not for the preacher. The 'door' for the opening of which he desires them to pray can hardly be the 'door of his lips,' as some have thought. It is plainly an opportunity for speaking. Apparently the λόγος of Ephesians (ἵνα μοι δοθῇ λόγος) means much the same, *i.e.* 'a chance of speaking.' What is the "'*mystery*' *of Christ*"? L. says it is the admission of the Gentiles to the New Covenant. That certainly had led (I mean, the bold preaching of it) to the Apostle's own imprisonment. If only he would have been a Jew and a Christian together, all would have been well for him. It was as a renegade he was attacked so bitterly, and his life so often sought. The interpretation of L. is borne out in part by chapter i. 26-29. In Ephesians, it would seem, the meaning is definitely broader. The whole revelation of Christ is essentially μυστήριον. The 'coupling chain' there does not figure as due to the preaching of the μυστήριον; not *because of* that, but *on behalf of* that is he 'an ambassador in a chain'; and the 'chain' (as I should hold) merely points a paradox. However, even here one can't feel sure that τὸ μυστήριον τοῦ Χριστοῦ should be limited as suggested. The language of chapter i. is more clearly defined by far.

In Ephesians the objects of the intercession for which the Apostle asks are definitely two (as L. observes): first, that opportunity be given; next, that it be boldly used. The mention of 'boldness' comes there twice over, ἐν παρρησίᾳ (*v.* 19) and παρρησιάσωμαι (*v.* 20). Here it lurks in φανερώσω and in the closing phrase. If he has gone to prison for it, as he has, there is not much fear he will fail in courage now.

The next two verses deal with Christian bearing and conduct.

iv. 5. 6. "Behave yourselves wisely in regard to those 'outside.' Use you *opportunities*, as they come" (or, "make good use of your *time*"). "Let your discourse be always *winning*, agreeably seasoned, so that you may *know* (without the telling) how you ought to answer *in every case*."

All this is application of the Lord Christ's famous rule, γίνεσθε οὖν φρόνιμοι ὡς οἱ ὄφεις καὶ ἀκέραιοι ὡς αἱ περιστεραί ("*Be ye therefore wary as the serpent and innocent as the dove*"). The σοφία (it will be seen) is a wholly different σοφία from that we had just now in iii. 16. This is a 'wisdom' of discretion, in fact, a kind of φρόνησις. Οἱ ἔξω (L.) is a Jewish phrase. We have it with its antithesis (οἱ ἔσω, "*those within*") in 1 Cor. v. 12, 13. Josephus correspondingly uses οἱ ἔξωθεν for 'Gentiles.' 'And he gained credit with outsiders too,' he says of King Herod, *Ant.* xv. 9, 2 (εὔκλεια δὲ καὶ παρὰ τῶν ἔξωθεν ἦν). The phrase τὸν καιρὸν ἐξαγοραζόμενοι obviously means what the paraphrase says. But how does it come to mean it? In the LXX of Dan. ii. 8 King Nebuchadnezzar says to the Chaldeans (who had innocently asked that they might be told the vision, which he said was 'gone from him'), "*I know of a certainty that ye would gain time*" (ἐπ' ἀληθείας οἶδα ἐγὼ ὅτι *καιρὸν ὑμεῖς ἐξαγοράζετε*). The curious phrase must mean what the English says, though *χρόνον* would have been far more natural Greek than *καιρόν*. Ἐ*ξαγοράζειν* in such usages means to 'buy up' or 'buy eagerly.' It might also mean 'buy off.' It does so in Gal. iii. 13, "Christ *redeemed* us from the curse of the Law" (*ἐξηγόρασεν ἐκ τῆς κατάρας τοῦ νόμου*). But 'opportunities' are not '*redeemed*' in any accurate sense of the word. They are (by wise people) eagerly seized. And that is what is demanded here. The sense of 'purchase,' in fact, is weak and all but vanished: the sense of 'eagerness' is strong, though in origin secondary. In Ephes. v. 16 a reason is subjoined for this eagerness not to let opportunities slip. It is "*because the days are evil.*" Therefore, "*while we have time,*" we must use it. "*The night cometh when no one can work*" (St. John ix. 4). Of course it may be urged that '*time*' (if *καιρός* is equivalent to *χρόνος*, as in Daniel *l.c.*) is 'redeemed' if it be not lost; but that is putting a somewhat forced construction on the word. It is not at all the same thing as the 'redemption' in L.'s quotation, *διὰ μιᾶς ὥρας τὴν αἰώνιον κόλασιν ἐξαγοραζόμενοι*, said of martyrs who, by one short hour of anguish, 'buy off' for themselves an eternity of chastisement. Our "*redeem*" comes from the Vulgate, *redimentes tempus*. In *v.* 6 *λόγος* means merely 'speech,' 'conversation.' The *χάρις* ("grace") of *ἐν χάριτι* is not the *χάρις* of theology. It is the *χάρις* of daily life. It means merely 'attractiveness.' "Let your speech ever be *with attractiveness.*" *Χάρις* is a very chameleon of a word. For indeed it may either lie in the thing perceived or in the percipient. Broadly speaking, it means four things (as the Dean of Wells has laid down in his admirable commentary on Ephesians):

(1) Attractiveness.

(2) The impression produced by attractiveness, *i.e.* favourable regard.

(3) The product of 'favourable regard,' a concrete 'favour.'

(4) The result produced by a 'favour,' a sense of gratitude.

Here it bears the first sense of all. Christian speech is not to be 'pious' or 'pietistic.' It is just to be 'winning,' 'attractive.' Such was Our Lord's own speech. The people "*hung on His lips*" (ἐξεκρέμετο, St. Luke xix. 48) in their eagerness to hear what He had to say. The expression ἅλατι ἠρτυμένος more nearly defines ἐν χάριτι. It only means "*well seasoned*" (literally, 'salted with salt'). Compare the language of St. Luke xiv. 34, "*But if the salt turn insipid, wherewith shall it be seasoned?*" (ἐὰν δὲ τὸ ἅλας μωρανθῇ, ἐν τίνι ἀρτυθήσεται;) 'Gracious and attractive' would be the sense of it. We are not concerned (I think) with the double function of salt, as at once a preservative and a source of flavour. The word is used as it would normally be in Greek, in connexion with speech, whether written or spoken. Only Christian *sal* will differ of necessity from heathen *sal*. That was evil, oftentimes degenerating (as L. observes) into mere obscenity. Think of Aristophanes at his worst! Εἰδέναι ὑμᾶς is (in construction) like the λαλῆσαι of *v.* 3. When the word is used accurately it means the knowledge of intuition—the knowledge which is not taught, but simply comes. Ἑνὶ ἑκάστῳ ("each single one," paraphrased above 'in every case') reminds us that people cannot be dealt with by wholesale methods. Each must be treated as his nature demands. St. Paul, in his own work, showed himself a master in the art of adaptability. Cf. 1 Cor. ix. 22. There is nothing in Ephesians which reproduces this special counsel.

We now pass on to personal matters. The first is a statement about Tychicus, whom we know from Acts xx. 4 to have been himself an 'Asian.' He was one of the band of 'disciples' of his own and 'delegates' of the Churches, who went with the Apostle to Jerusalem to take the alms collected in Macedonia and Achaia for the poor at Jerusalem. In Acts he is closely coupled with Trophimus the Ephesian (so called in xxi. 29) and, consequently, may have been an Ephesian too. From Ephes. vi. 21 (a passage very closely similar to this) we should conclude that he was probably entrusted with that 'circular' letter. The name recurs again much later in the Pastorals: in Tit. iii. 12, "When I send Artemas to thee or Tychicus, make haste to come to me at Nicopolis"; and 2 Tim. iv. 12, "Tychicus I have despatched (ἀπέστειλα) *to Ephesus.*" Plainly he was one of St. Paul's regular staff, or aides-de-camp. The name is found on inscriptions, but is not so common as Onesimus or Trophimus (L.). Tychicus is not on the same level of importance or dignity as Timothy. The latter appears in the salutations of Philippians, Colossians, and Philemon, coupled with the Apostle himself. Tychicus only occurs in messages.

iv. 7-9. "All my concerns shall be made known to you by Tychicus, the beloved brother, and faithful minister and fellow-servant 'in the Lord.' Him I am sending to you for this very purpose, that you may get to know all about me, and that he may comfort your hearts—and Onesimus the faithful and beloved brother, who is one of yourselves. They shall make known to you all the news of Rome."

In Ephesians Tychicus is described as "the beloved brother and faithful *minister in the Lord*" (πιστὸς διάκονος ἐν Κυρίῳ). Was he technically a 'deacon'—'deacons' are mentioned as Church officers in Phil. i. 1, the earliest official mention, unless Phœbe was really a deaconess, Rom. xvi. 1—or was he one of those whose 'ministry' was personal to the Apostle (see Acts xix. 22, where Timothy and Erastes are mentioned as δύο τῶν διακονούντων αὐτῷ, "two of those that ministered to him")? The verb διακονεῖν (remember) is also associated with Onesimus (Philemon 13) in its purely personal sense. L. tells us that the title σύνδουλος was a customary form of address from a Bishop to a Deacon. Epaphras is called in i. 7 "*our beloved fellow-servant,*" and also πιστὸς ὑπὲρ ἡμῶν διάκονος τοῦ Χριστοῦ; from which one would be inclined to conclude that Tychicus was an evangelist and preacher, and that his 'ministry' and 'service' was *to Christ Himself.*

I do not think he can have been an officer of any stated Christian body. If he helped the great Missionary in his all-important work, that would constitute him 'minister' and 'fellow-servant' too 'in the Lord' in a very real sense. We should gather that he was entirely at St. Paul's disposal, to use as he should choose. As an 'Asian' himself he was a natural emissary to send to Asian Churches. Where the ἐν Κυρίῳ belongs, it is hard to say. L. would take it with πιστὸς διάκονος καὶ συνδοῦλος. It is not needed for ἀδελφός (he says): that is complete in itself. Ἔπεμψα is 'epistolary,' "*I am sending.*" Τὰ περὶ ἡμῶν, I believe, means much the same as τὰ κατ' ἐμέ. It was about St. Paul they wished to know. Aristarchus and the rest were of small account. About St. Paul he could give them altogether encouraging news. Compare the Apostle's own statements in Phil. i. 12 ff. There τὰ κατ' ἐμέ bears a rather different force. About Onesimus, the runaway slave, we learn all there is to know (apart from Church traditions) in the letter to Philemon. Did he take this Epistle straight to Colossæ, or did he wait till Tychicus could come with him and support him in what must have been a somewhat trying meeting? In that case they would have journeyed together from Ephesus, and would have passed through Laodicea (dropping a copy of Ephesians there) *en route* to Colossæ. The phrase σὺν Ὀνησίμῳ may seem to point to a journey in fellowship, but not inevitably. Onesimus (observe) is no διάκονος in the sense that Tychicus is. He is merely a private soldier in the armies of the Lord. He is called what all of us should wish to be called, "*a faithful and beloved brother.*" "*Who is one of yourselves.*" This is the way the Apostle speaks of a runaway slave. Compare the language used in Philemon 11, "*my child whom I have begotten in my bonds*" (τοῦ ἐμοῦ τέκνου ὃν ἐγέννησα ἐν τοῖς δεσμοῖς), and again, "*no longer as a slave, but more than a slave, a brother beloved*" (οὐκέτι ὡς δοῦλον ἀλλὰ ὑπὲρ δοῦλον, ἀδελφὸν ἀγαπητόν). That is how his old master is asked to welcome him on his return.

Πάντα τὰ ὧδε depends for its meaning on what we conceive to have been the place of writing. Once it was Cæsarea; for a long time it was Rome; now some have evolved from within themselves an imprisonment at Ephesus. Rome seems to me far more likely: accordingly I venture to say so.

Now come the messages of greeting. There are none at all in Ephesians, as one would naturally expect in a letter not meant for one, but for many 'churches' (to use the term which St. Paul by now had given up using, or even appearing to use—seeing the Church is only one). The names, with one omission, are found in Philemon too.

The first is Aristarchus. Now he was a Thessalonian, but had been with St. Paul at Ephesus at the time of the riot (see Acts xix. 29), when he had had an alarming experience. He also was one of those who accompanied St. Paul to Jerusalem on his last beneficent visit in Acts xx. However, Acts xxvii. 2 is the most telling mention of him.

From that we learn that he actually shipped with Paul the Prisoner on his adventurous voyage to Rome, in company with Luke. Professor Ramsay thinks that they must have gone *as slaves.* If so, Aristarchus certainly qualified there and then for the honourable 'addition' ὁ συναιχμαλωτός μου ("my fellow-prisoner"). His Ephesian sojourn must have made him familiar to the Colossians. He may conceivably have helped in their evangelisation. In Philemon his mention occurs only amid a string of names.

The next person mentioned is "Mark, the *cousin* of Barnabas." The word ἀνεψιός by derivation is said to mean 'one having a common grandfather,' or 'joint-grandson.' The sense 'cousin' is the LXX sense (so L.). The meaning 'nephew' is later.

How many 'Marks' are there in N.T.—one, or two, or three? Is the 'John' surnamed Mark and son of Mary of Acts xii. 12, who was taken by Saul and Barnabas back to Antioch with them at the close of their mission of charity (Acts xii. 25), the same as the 'John' whom they had as their "*minister*" (ὑπηρέτης, that is, 'attendant') when they went forth on the first Mission Journey (Acts xiii. 5), and, accordingly, the same with the 'John' who basely deserted them (ἀποχωρήσας) at Perga (xiii. 13), and angered Paul so deeply that he absolutely refused to have him as a travelling companion, when Barnabas was so anxious to take him (Acts xv. 37)? All this seems probable, and the mention of a relationship between the 'Mark' of Colossians and St. Paul's old fellow-worker suggests that he too must be the same as the 'John' of Acts. These considerations would establish the identity of the 'Mark' of Acts, Colossians, and Philemon. But what of the 'Mark' of 2 Timothy, of whom it is said, "Take Mark and bring him with thee, for he is useful *to me* for ministering" (or possibly, "for he is *in my judgment* a useful minister")? ἔστιν γάρ μοι εὔχρηστος εἰς διακονίαν; Is he too to be accounted the same? Most people would certainly say 'Yes.' There remains yet one other 'Mark' of N.T. Scriptures, the 'Mark' of 1 Peter v. 13, "The Church that is in 'Babylon' salutes you and *Mark my son*" (καὶ Μάρκος ὁ υἱός μου). Is this "*son*" of St. Peter, too, the old 'John Mark' of the other passages? And what about the 'Mark' of Eusebius' tale (*H.E.* ii. 15, 16), who is found at Rome with St. Peter in the days of the Emperor Claudius—before ever St. Paul reached there—and at the earnest intercession of the faithful produces his written 'memoir' (ὑπόμνημα) of the sacred Story; which Mark is also identified with the Mark of 1 Peter v. in the Eusebian tradition, and declared to have preached the Gospel *first* (whatever that may mean) in Egypt, and to have organised the Church at Alexandria?

L. says that the statement in Eusebius about the Apostle Peter's early arrival at Rome is 'irreconcilable with the notices in the Apostolic writings.'[1] For the rest, he is quite content to

[1] Harnack thinks otherwise. He considers it possible, though beyond the reach of proof.

regard all these several 'Marks' as one and the same. The Mark who is 'son' of St. Peter is the same as the 'Mark' we have here. He is in Rome already, and the 'Babylon' of 1 Peter is probably Rome too. How his allegiance was transferred from the one Apostle to the other must remain a mystery; but it probably was so. Maybe St. Paul was already dead. That the Gospel of St. Mark was written at Rome is matter of early tradition. Yet the belief in the tradition is not without its difficulties.

Mark, then, the old John Mark, sends his salutations to Colossæ. A statement is made about him which is somewhat puzzling: "*About whom you have been given orders* (ἐλάβετε ἐντολάς): *if he shall come to you, receive him.*" It seems evident that the writer anticipated in the readers some little unwillingness to welcome Mark as his friend could wish. That we can understand. Maybe it was only lately that he and the Prisoner Apostle had effected a reconciliation and in the parts of Asia his reputation might not have emerged as yet from its temporary eclipse. But the real trouble comes about the περὶ οὗ ἐλάβετε ἐντολάς. I feel absolutely certain the ἐλάβετε cannot be an 'epistolary' aorist. That aorist only applies to verbs which have to do with the writer himself, when writing. Ἔπεμψα is 'epistolary,' but ἐλάβετε could not possibly be. It follows that communications had passed already between St. Paul and the Colossian Church. Already he had bidden them welcome Mark, if he should come. With characteristic anxiety he reminds them of that 'commandment.' Whether δέξασθε be read or δέξασθαι makes no sort of difference. The purport of the *orders* must be as stated.

Yet another name is mentioned, "*Jesus, called Justus*"; and then we are informed that all the three are "*of the circumcision.*" 'Jesus' would be, of course, and Mark (for his cousin is a Levite), but one is rather surprised to find that Aristarchus is too. Acts xix. 29 does not prepare us for it. But perhaps he is not meant for inclusion with the two others. Jesus Justus is found only here. He is omitted in Philemon. L. gives many instances of Jews called 'Justus.' There are two others in N.T., the Joseph Barsabbas of Acts i. 23, and the Titius Justus of Acts xviii. 7. About these two (or these three) the writer has somewhat to say.

iv. 11 (part). "These only are fellow-workers towards the Kingdom of God; they have been a comfort to me."

The Jewish Christians at Rome were a trouble to St. Paul. Such are probably the persons referred to in Phil. i. 15-17. "*But others proclaim Christ from* (a spirit of) *contention; not sincerely, thinking to arouse affliction for my bonds.*" Amongst them the Apostle declares he found only these genuine helpers (συνεργοί); maybe the others only *talked.* The οἵτινες merely means "*people, who have been.*" The relative is employed in a non-classical way to introduce a new statement. The sense of εἰς τὴν βασιλείαν should be noticed: it means (as given above) "*towards the Kingdom,*" *i.e.* towards the realisation of the Kingdom.

In the beautiul little letter of consolation (*Greek Papyri*, Milligan, No. 38) the verb παρηγορεῖν is used as the noun is here. 'Yet truly one can do nothing in the face of things like this. So comfort yourselves (παρηγορεῖτε ἑαυτούς).'

But let us before going further provide a paraphrase of the verses with which we are concerned:

iv. 10-14. "Greeting to you from Aristarchus my fellow-prisoner, and from Mark the cousin of Barnabas, about whom you have received charges, 'if he come to you, give him welcome'; and from Jesus, who is called Justus—men of the Circumcision.

These only join in the work of forwarding God's Kingdom. *They* have been to me a comfort.

Greeting to you from Epaphras, who is one of yourselves, a (true) servant of Jesus Christ, evermore *wrestling* on your behalf in his prayers that you *may be established* perfect and *complete* in all the Will of God. For I bear him witness that he is much concerned for you and for the folks at Laodicea and the folks at Hierapolis.

Greetings from Luke the beloved physician and from Demas."

The Epaphras of *v.* 12 is the Epaphras of i. 7. There he is called "*our beloved fellow-servant*" (ἀγαπητοῦ συνδούλου), so that St. Paul is clearly ready to couple him with himself. Commendation could go no further. Although the name is the same, for 'Epaphras' is only an abbreviation of 'Epaphroditus' (a singular name for a Christian), he is not to be identified with the Epaphroditus of

Philippians, who bore the welcome offerings of the Macedonian Church to Rome, and fell seriously ill there and had to be sent home. That 'Epaphras' is called συνεργός and συστρατιώτης ("*fellow-worker and comrade in arms*"): he does not attain to σύνδουλος and δοῦλος Ἰησοῦ Χριστοῦ. The Apostle calls himself by the latter title often: it is his chosen designation. The only other Christian he calls so is Timothy (in Philippians). In LXX ἀγωνίζεσθαι merely means 'contend' or 'strive.' All sense of 'agony' is gone from it. I think we must distinguish the γενόμενος ἐν ἀγωνίᾳ of the Passion in St. Luke from our ἀγωνιζόμενος altogether. It would have been a different case with the participle before us had ἀγωνίζεσθαι been the verb employed of the mysterious stranger in Genesis xxxii. 24, who "*wrestled*" with the Patriarch. There, however, it is ἐπάλαιεν, a decidedly technical word. Perhaps, therefore, "*always contending*" would be a safer rendering. Even ἀγωνιᾶν (a stronger form) means in papyrus letters no more than 'be anxious.' "*Stand fast*" (I hold) is not a proper rendering for σταθῆτε. The word is a true passive in such connexions and means "*be established.*" Compare Rom. xiv. 4. "To his own owner he *standeth*, or he falleth (τῷ ἰδίῳ κυρίῳ στήκει ἢ πίπτει); but *he shall be established* (σταθήσεται δέ), for the Lord can establish (στῆσαι) him." The same sense, also in the future (the future of the same tense-stem), is found in 2 Cor. xiii. 1. Rev. vi. 17 is probably the same, for ἐστάθην naturally means either 'I took my stand' (deponent), or 'I was set up' (passive). In an Ephesian parallel we have *στῆναι*, not *σταθῆναι*. That is correctly rendered 'stand':

"Therefore take ye up the armour of God that ye may be able to withstand in the evil day, and having accomplished all (ἅπαντα κατεργασάμενοι) to stand (στῆναι)." (Ephes. vi. 13.)

The effect, to be sure, is the same, but it is reached in different ways. The "*be established*" and "*stand*" refer to the final issue of things. Τέλειοι does not here mean 'mature,' 'full-grown' (as it does in certain passages), but indubitably 'perfect' ('flawless'), as in Christ's famous saying, and in chapter i. 28. Πεπληροφορημένοι might perfectly well mean "*fully persuaded*" (as L. would render it). But it makes no kind of sense. The meaning 'accomplish' is not disputed, nor is 'fill.' Instances of both are supplied by L. In 2 Tim. iv. we find "*fulfil thy ministry*" (τὴν διακονίαν σου πληροφόρησον), and again, "*that by my means the preaching might be completed* (τὸ κήρυγμα πληροφορηθῇ) *and all the nations might hear.*" This latter comes nearest to the sense I desiderate here. A Christian, I conceive, is "*completed*" when the work of the Holy Spirit is accomplished in his heart. In James i. 4 we have ὁλόκληροι associated with τέλειοι with much the same signification. Ἐν παντὶ θελήματι may mean "*in everything willed by God,*" but seeing that in St. Paul God's 'will' is only one in a general way (as in the Lord's Prayer), it seems to me wiser and better to render "*in all the will of God.*" The absence of the article need not trouble us. The addition of the words "*in* all the will of God" to the participle "*complete*" I admit is difficult. But "*convinced in every will*" is at least as difficult, and the illustrations in L.'s note to support his rendering are very unconvincing.

It is curious to observe, in regard to *v.* 13, that it is the only place where πόνος occurs in St. Paul. Therefore it is of necessity not easy to be sure of any rendering. The words for 'toil' in St. Paul are κόπος and μόχθος. Πονεῖν is used for 'to be troubled' in a papyrus letter.

Laodicea and Hierapolis (the latter only mentioned here) were probably a part of Epaphras' 'cure.' He had preached the Gospel, no doubt, in all three. 'Lucas' (Luke) is the man of Acts. He journeyed with St. Paul to Jerusalem on his final visit; he probably ministered to him during the Cæsarea captivity; he sailed with him to Rome. Whether he had been with the Apostle in Rome all the time we cannot tell. He is not mentioned in the Philippian letter. From that Bishop Lightfoot infers that he was not. Only three times does his name occur in Holy Writ, in Colossians, in Philemon, and in 2 Timothy—unless indeed he be the 'Lucius' of Rom. xvi. He was almost certainly a Gentile, and probably an Antiochene (as ancient tradition avers). Ramsay's contention as to the meaning of the phrase in Euseb. *H.E.* iii. 4, γένος ὢν τῶν ἀπ' Ἀντιοχείας, is disproved by a similar usage in a papyrus (Milligan, No. 20, "A Contract of Apprenticeship"), ἀμφότεροι τῶν ἀπ' Ὀξυρύγχων πόλεως, which can only mean 'both Oxyrhynchites by birth.'

St. Luke's services to the Apostle, extending over many years, had been of incalculable worth to that none too vigorous man; and so they were to the end. No wonder he styles him here "*the beloved physician.*" None had better reason to call him so. L. would render "*the physician, the beloved one,*" in part influenced by the Gospel analogy of ὁ υἱός μου, ὁ ἀγαπητός, "*My Son, My Beloved.*" But there the "*Beloved*" is a prophetic title: here the conditions are other.

As for poor Demas, the same poor creature who "*left*" St. Paul "*in the lurch*" in those last sad days of the second imprisonment, when Luke was so true to him (Δημᾶς γάρ με ἐγκατέλιπεν, ἀγαπήσας τὸν νῦν αἰῶνα, 2 Tim. iv. 10), L. bids us note that he has no honorific mention. There is no good to be said of him: he is just a name —no more. A mention equally brief is found of him in Philemon (*v.* 24). He may have been a Colossian. 'Demas,' like 'Lucas,' is a shortened name; it may stand for 'Demetrius.' Any kind of long termination was abbreviated into -as.

The letter goes on, and ends:

iv. 15-18. "Greet the brethren at Laodicea, and Nymphas and the 'Church' that is in † *their* † house. And when the letter has been read before you, cause that it be read also in the assembly of the Laodiceans; and mind that you too read the Laodicean letter. Moreover, say to Archippus, Look to the ministry thou hast been delivered 'in the Lord,' that thou discharge it aright.

The greeting is by the hand of me, Paul. Bear in mind my bonds. God's Grace be with you!"

This last section suggests several very interesting questions. The "*brethren at Laodicea*" one naturally takes to mean 'all the "Church" at Laodicea,' that is, all of the *one Christian Body* that may chance to be living there. It might mean Colossian Christians, who are staying at Laodicea, but it does not seem to be a likely hypothesis. The "*and* Nymphas" is curious. Does it mean "*especially* Nymphas"? Or did Nymphas not live in Laodicea but (say) at a villa outside? 'Nymphas' is probably 'Nymphodorus,' and a man. Some MSS. make it 'Nympha,' a woman. But the form Νύμφαν in that case should rather be Νύμφην. "*The 'Church' in . . . house*" is puzzling, because the MSS. read some *αὐτῶν*, some *αὐτοῦ*, some *αὐτῆς*. B. reads *αὐτῆς*. This is the reading of W. H. Nestle reads it too. Tischendorf reads *αὐτῶν*, which is also L.'s choice. The latter argues that *αὐτοῦ* and *αὐτῆς* are both natural corrections. If *αὐτῶν* be correct, another name has probably dropped out, the name of Nymphas' wife. In Rom. xvi. 5 and in 1 Cor. xvi. 19 the 'Church' in the house of Aquila and Prisca is mentioned (in the former place the wife coming first). In Philemon we have mention of the 'Church' in Philemon's house. He would seem to have lived at Colossæ, seeing Onesimus came from there, and the Archippus greeted in the private letter (with Philemon and Apphia) is mentioned in a message here, being presumably Philemon's son.

St. Paul uses these several expressions, 'the Church,' or 'the saints,' or 'the brethren' in 'so-and-so's house,' apparently at will.

"*The letter*" is this letter (as in Rom. xvi. 22). Ἐν τῇ Λαοδικέων ἐκκλησίᾳ I think means "in the *assembly* of the Laodiceans"; that is, the term ἐκκλησία no longer means 'the Church,' but merely the gathering of Church members. The verb ἀναγνωσθῇ implies (quite apart from the context) public reading. The phrase τὴν ἐκ Λαοδικίας has been very variously interpreted. It is a characteristic Greek brachylogy, by which 'the letter from Laodicea' means 'the letter you will find *at* Laodicea, and have to get *from* there.' Any Greek syntax will illustrate this.

L. provides a wonderful catalogue of various suggestions. They number no less than fourteen, but the more part can be rejected without the faintest hesitation. The letter in question was written beyond a doubt *to* Laodicea, and almost certainly by St. Paul himself. The only question is, Have we it still? The answer is Yes: it most probably is the letter we call Ephesians. There is every indication of that being a 'circular' letter, and a copy would have been dropped at Laodicea by the messenger on his way to Colossæ. Moreover, one copy of the letter would have served for both the Churches—and for Hierapolis too.

Certain MSS. (be it observed) contain an apocryphal Epistle entitled *Ad Laodicenses.* It is characterised by L. as 'a mere cento of Pauline phrases strung together without any definite connexion or any clear subject.' This curious compilation he has rendered into Greek. Both versions will be found in his edition of Colossians.

The mention of Archippus in *v.* 17 is deeply interesting. From Philemon we should gather that he lived with that Christian householder and with "*Apphia our sister*," being possibly their son. His "*ministry*" (*διακονίαν*) is not to be regarded as an actual 'diaconate.' He may have been a Presbyter of the Colossian community. Plainly, whatever it was, he was not so zealous in its discharge as comported both with his office and with his Christian profession. Ἣν *παρέλαβες* contains no indication from whom he had obtained it. It may have been indeed from St. Paul himself, but I think if it had been so the Apostle would have mentioned it. No doubt it had been conferred with 'laying on of hands.' As for the interpretation given of the term *διακονίᾳ*, be it noted that in 2 Timothy St. Paul's famous lieutenant is bidden in almost identical terms to "*discharge his ministry*" (*τὴν διακονίαν σου πληροφόρησον*), and he was assuredly not a 'deacon,' technically speaking, at the time. Βλέπε . . . *ἵνα πληροῖς* shows us how we are to fill up mentally the elliptical expression in the verse next above, *ἵνα καὶ ὑμεῖς ἀναγνῶτε.*

When the writer says in *v.* 18 that the 'greeting' is autograph, he means merely that verse, no more. St. Paul, as is well known, did not write his letters with his own hand—probably not because of weakness of eyes, but merely because he was too important a person to do so. In Rom. xvi. is preserved the name of one *amanuensis*, "*I Tertius* who am writing the latter salute you Christianly" (ἀσπάζομαι ὑμᾶς ἐγὼ Τέρτιος ὁ γράψας τὴν ἐπιστολὴν ἐν Κυρίῳ, Rom. xvi. 22). This autograph authentification of genuine Pauline documents begins with 2 Thessalonians. There we read, "The salutation (is) by the hand of me, Paul: it is a mark in every letter. *This is how I write*" (οὕτως γράφω), 2 Thess. iii. 17. There, I think, we must conclude that the "*so I write*" calls attention to the well-known hand. In Galatians there is, of course, a whole section of autograph (vi. 11-end), and that, to be sure, may be earlier than even 2 Thessalonians. But I do not think it is. The Apostolic practice is referred to in 1 Corinthians, Colossians, 2 Thessalonians, of extant letters.

As for "*remember my bonds*," the reader must compare Philemon 9, "Yet for love's sake I rather beg, being such an one as Paul the aged, and now even *the prisoner of Christ Jesus*" (τοιοῦτος ὢν ὡς Παῦλος πρεσβύτης νυνὶ δὲ καὶ δέσμιος Χριστοῦ Ἰησοῦ); and Ephes. iv. 1, "I beseech you then, *I the prisoner of the Lord*" (παρακαλῶ οὖν ὑμᾶς ἐγὼ ὁ δέσμιος ἐν Κυρίῳ). He does not ask for their pity, but his imprisonment does constitute an additional claim on their obedience.

The very brief form of 'the Grace' (found only here and in the Pastorals) is the note of a late letter. The χάρις, no doubt, is the χάρις of Jesus Christ. We repeat and hear the words so very often that we hardly stop to think what their meaning is. 'Grace' in the sense of the Latin *gratia* and the word as used in English is not common in N.T. Some aver it is not there at all. Here I should say the sense is "*God's favour, in Jesus Christ, be with you all!*" The brevity of the expression marks its familiarity for the readers.

# THE ENGLISH TEXT OF THE EPISTLE

### Version of 1611.

i. 1. Paul, an apostle of Jesus Christ by the will of God, and Timotheus our brother,

2. To the saints and faithful brethren in Christ which are at Colosse: Grace be unto you, and peace, from God our Father and the Lord Jesus Christ.

3. We give thanks to God and the Father of our Lord Jesus Christ, praying always for you,

4. Since we heard of your faith in Christ Jesus, and of the love which ye have to all the saints,

5. For the hope which is laid up for you in heaven, whereof ye heard before in the word of the truth of the gospel;

6. Which is come unto you, as it is in all the world; and bringeth forth fruit, as it doth also in you, since the day ye heard of it, and knew the grace of God in truth:

7. As ye also learned of Epaphras our dear fellowservant, who is for you a faithful minister of Christ;

8. Who also declared unto us your love in the Spirit.

9. For this cause we also, since the day we heard it, do not cease

### Paraphrase.

i. 1, 2. Paul by divine "will" an "apostle" of Christ Jesus and Timothy the "brother" to the "saints" that are in Colossæ—I mean the faithful brothers "in Christ"; grace be to you and peace from God our Father.

i. 3, 4. On every occasion, when I pray for you, I thank the Divine Father of Our Lord Jesus Christ, because I have heard tell of your faith as Christian men and your love towards all the saints,

i. 5-8. Because of the Hope which is laid up for you in the heavens; of which you were told long since by the message of the true Gospel; which has come to you, as it also is all the world over; bearing fruit and ever extending—as it also does in you, since the day that you were told of it, and came to know the Grace of God, as it really is; as you learned from Epaphras, our beloved fellowservant, who is on my behalf a faithful minister of God's Christ; who also has showed me how you love as spiritual folks should.

i. 9, 10. For this cause I too, since I was told, have not

to pray for you, and to desire that ye might be filled with the knowledge of his will in all wisdom and spiritual understanding ;

10. That ye might walk worthy of the Lord unto all pleasing, being fruitful in every good work, and increasing in the knowledge of God ;

ceased praying for you and making supplication, to the intent you may be filled with the fuller knowledge of His will and be altogether wise and spiritually understanding ; that your walk may be worthy of the Lord in all subservience ; and may bear fruit in every good doing, and that you may grow through growing knowledge of God.

11. Strengthened with all might, according to his glorious power, unto all patience and long-suffering with joyfulness ;

12. Giving thanks unto the Father, which hath made us meet to be partakers of the inheritance of the saints in light :

i. 11, 12. That you be empowered with all power, after His all-glorious, conquering might, so as to be altogether brave and altogether patient — aye, and joyful too ! Giving thanks to the Great Father, that hath made us believers fit for a share in the lot of the Saints, that stand in Light.

13. Who hath delivered us from the power of darkness, and hath translated us into the kingdom of his dear Son :

14. In whom we have redemption through his blood, even the forgiveness of sins :

i. 13, 14. Who has rescued us from the reign of darkness and has transferred us to the Kingdom of the Son of His love ; in Whom we have our redemption, the remission of our sins.

15. Who is the image of the invisible God, the firstborn of every creature :

16. For by him were all things created, that are in heaven, and that are in earth, visible and invisible, whether they be thrones, or dominions, or principalities, or powers : all things were created by him, and for him :

i. 15, 16. Who is the manifest Likeness of God invisible ; begotten before all Creation ; for in Him were all things created, in heaven and upon earth ; things visible and things invisible ; whether "thrones," whether "lordships," whether "dominions," whether "rules" — all things created are through Him, and unto Him.

17. And he is before all things, and by him all things consist.

i. 17. And He is before all things and everything that is owes its mode of existence to Him.

18. And he is the head of the body, the church : who is the beginning, the firstborn from the dead ; that in all things he might have the preeminence.

i. 18. And He is the "Head" of the Body, the Church ; seeing He is its source and beginning, first-begotten from the dead, that everywhere He may prove in Himself pre-eminent.

19. For it pleased the Father that in him should all fulness dwell;

20. And, having made peace through the blood of his cross, by him to reconcile all things unto himself; by him, I say, whether they be things in earth, or things in heaven.

21. And you, that were sometime alienated and enemies in your mind by wicked works, yet now hath he reconciled.

22. In the body of his flesh through death, to present you holy and unblameable and unreproveable in his sight:

23. If ye continue in the faith grounded and settled, and be not moved away from the hope of the gospel, which ye have heard, and which was preached to every creature which is under heaven; whereof I Paul am made a minister;

24. Who now rejoice in my sufferings for you, and fill up that which is behind of the afflictions of Christ in my flesh for his body's sake, which is the church:

25. Whereof I am made a minister, according to the dispensation of God which is given to me for you, to fulfil the word of God;

26. Even the mystery which hath been hid from ages and from generations, but now is made manifest to his saints:

27. To whom God would make known what is the riches of the glory of this mystery among the Gentiles; which is Christ in you, the hope of glory:

28. Whom we preach, warning

i. 19, 20. For in Him was He pleased there should dwell all the Plenitude (of the Godhead) bodily, and through Him to reconcile "all things" unto Himself, having made peace through the blood of His cross—by Him (I say) whether things on earth or things in the heavens.

i. 21, 22. Aye, and you that once were estranged and enemies in disposition, while you worked your evil works—but now you have been reconciled by the Body of His incarnation—(He hath been pleased) to display you holy and blameless before Him and beyond the reach of any charge.

i. 23. Provided that ye stay on in Faith, firm founded and stedfast, and are not inclined to move from the hope of the Gospel which ye heard, which has been proclaimed in every corner of the creation under heaven, whereof I Paul have been an instrument.

i. 24. Oh, now I rejoice in my sufferings for your sakes, and so far as in me lies fill up in my poor person what is lacking in Christ's afflictions for His Body's sake, which is the Church.

i. 25-29. Wherein I became an instrument in accordance with the heavenly "stewardship" which was committed to me, to reach as far as you, that I should preach God's "Word" completely—the "wonderful truth" that was hidden away from ages and generations, but now has been plainly shown to His saints; to whom God has been pleased to make known the grandeur and the glory of this revelation amongst the nations, that is, Christ in you, the great Hope of Glory.

every man, and teaching every man in all wisdom ; that we may present every man perfect in Christ Jesus :

29. Whereunto I also labour, striving according to his working, which worketh in me mightily.

Whom we proclaim abroad, warning every man and instructing every man in every "wisdom," that we may display every man fully initiate "in Christ." To which end I also toil and strive in accordance with the power that worketh in me mightily.

ii. 1. For I would that ye knew what great conflict I have for you, and for them at Laodicea, and for as many as have not seen my face in the flesh ;

2. That their hearts might be comforted, being knit together in love, and unto all riches of the full assurance of understanding, to the acknowledgment of the mystery of God, and of the Father, and of Christ ;

3. In whom are hid all the treasures of wisdom and knowledge.

ii. 1-3. For I would have you know what a struggle I have for you and the people at Laodicea—in fact, for all that have not seen my face in bodily presence ; (praying) that their hearts be comforted and that they be knit together in love and (attain) to all the wealth of the fulness of understanding, unto a fuller knowledge of the "mystery" of God, CHRIST that is, in Whom are all the stores of "wisdom" and "knowledge," hidden away.

4. And this I say, lest any man should beguile you with enticing words.

5. For though I be absent in the flesh, yet am I with you in the spirit, joying and beholding your order, and the stedfastness of your faith in Christ.

ii. 4, 5. I say it for fear any should delude you with specious talk. For although I am away in bodily presence yet in spirit I am with you, rejoicing (in you) and beholding your orderly array, the solid front presented by your faith towards Christ.

6. As ye have therefore received Christ Jesus the Lord, so walk ye in him :

7. Rooted and built up in him, and stablished in the faith, as ye have been taught, abounding therein with thanksgiving.

ii. 6, 7. As then you were instructed about "the Christ," (that He is) Jesus the LORD, (so) walk in Him ; firmrooted (in Him) and evermore "built up" in Him, and made firmer in "the faith," as you were taught (it) ; abounding therein, with thanksgiving.

8. Beware lest any man spoil you through philosophy and vain deceit, after the tradition of men, after the rudiments of the world, and not after Christ.

ii. 8. Oh ! see that there shall be none who carries you off as prey, by means of his "philosophy" and vain deceit, following the traditions of men, following the "rudimentary teaching of the world," and not following Christ.

9. For in him dwelleth all the fulness of the Godhead bodily.

10. And ye are complete in him, which is the head of all principality and power:

11. In whom also ye are circumcised with the circumcision made without hands, in putting off the body of the sins of the flesh by the circumcision of Christ:

12. Buried with him in baptism, wherein also ye are risen with him through the faith of the operation of God, who hath raised him from the dead.

13. And you, being dead in your sins and the uncircumcision of your flesh, hath he quickened together with him, having forgiven you all trespasses;

14. Blotting out the handwriting of ordinances that was against us, which was contrary to us, and took it out of the way, nailing it to his cross;

15. And having spoiled principalities and powers, he made a shew of them openly, triumphing over them in it.

16. Let no man therefore judge you in meat, or in drink, or in respect of an holyday, or of the new moon, or of the sabbath days:

17. Which are a shadow of things to come; but the body is of Christ.

18. Let no man beguile you of your reward in a voluntary humility and worshipping of angels, intruding into those things which he hath not seen, vainly puffed up by his fleshly mind,

19. And not holding the Head, from which all the body by joints and bands having nourishment ministered, and knit together, in-

ii. 9. For in Him dwells all the fulness of the Godhead bodily.

ii. 10. And in Him you are fulfilled seeing He is the fountain-head of all authority and power.

ii. 11. Aye, in Him you have been circumcised with a circumcision supernatural, wherein you put off effectually the body's frailty, with the circumcision of Christ.

ii. 12. For you were buried with Him, in your Baptism, wherein also you were raised with Him through faith in the (mighty) working of God, Who raised Him from the dead.

ii. 13-15. Yes, you that were dead in your transgressions and your "carnal uncircumcision"—you, I say, God has "quickened" together with Christ, and has "forgiven" us all our transgressions, having "washed out" the "note of hand," that was against us, which stood in our way with its decrees; aye, He has taken it clean away, having nailed it to His Cross; stripping bare the principalities and powers, He has openly paraded them, leading them in triumph through It.

ii. 16, 17. Let not then any take you to task in regard to eating and drinking, or in respect of a feast or a new moon or a sabbath; which things are a (mere) shadow of "the things to come," whereas Christ is "the substance."

ii. 18, 19. Let no one beat you down, for all his will (to do so), by means of a humble-seeming subservience to angels. He is intruding upon spheres beyond his range of vision: he is filled with a vain conceit through his unillumined imaginings. Moreover, he does not hold fast the HEAD, from Whom all the body—thanks creaseth with the increase of God.

to its joints and ligatures—deriving its support and its increasing strength grows with the growth of God.

20. Wherefore if ye be dead with Christ from the rudiments of the world, why, as though living in the world, are ye subject to ordinances,

21. (Touch not; taste not; handle not;

22. Which all are to perish with the using;) after the commandments and doctrines of men?

23. Which things have indeed a shew of wisdom in will worship, and humility, and neglecting of the body; not in any honour to the satisfying of the flesh.

ii. 20-23. Oh! if you died with Christ and gave up the worldly rudiments, why as though living in the worldly sphere do you make rules for yourselves (such as) "Touch not, taste not, handle not"—(rules having to do with things) all of which pass away in the using, following ordinances and teachings which are (nothing more than) human? Such rules have a show of wisdom, dealing ruthlessly with the body through self-imposed austerities and (voluntary) humiliation, but are not of any value as against sensual indulgence.

iii. 1. If ye then be risen with Christ, seek those things which are above, where Christ sitteth on the right hand of God.

2. Set your affection on things above, not on things on the earth.

3. For ye are dead, and your life is hid with Christ in God.

4. When Christ, who is our life, shall appear, then shall ye also appear with him in glory.

iii. 1-4. If, I say, you were raised with Christ set your hearts on the realm above, where Christ is, seated high at God's right hand. Breathe the atmosphere of heaven and not of earth. For die you did, and your life is hidden away with Christ "in God." When Christ, our Life, shall be revealed, then shall you also be manifested with Him in glory.

5. Mortify therefore your members which are upon the earth; fornication, uncleanness, inordinate affection, evil concupiscence, and covetousness, which is idolatry:

6. For which things' sake the wrath of God cometh on the children of disobedience:

7. In the which ye also walked some time, when ye lived in them.

iii. 5-7. Kill then your earthly bodies! Fornication, uncleanness, sodomy (?), lewd desire,—(away with them all!) and greed, for it is idolatry; for which things' sake doth come the wrath of God. Wherein you too once walked, when your life was among them.

8. But now ye also put off all these; anger, wrath, malice, blasphemy, filthy communication out of your mouth.

9. Lie not one to another, see-

iii. 8-10. But now put you too away from yourselves every bit of it! anger, passion, malice, slander, vile talk upon your lips. Lie not to one another. Do off ing that ye have put off the old man with his deeds ;

10. And have put on the new man, which is renewed in knowledge after the image of him that created him :

the old man with his doings and do on the new, that evermore is freshened in growing knowledge, after the pattern of Him that made him.

11. Where there is neither Greek nor Jew, circumcision nor uncircumcision, Barbarian, Scythian, bond nor free : but Christ is all, and in all.

iii. 11. There can there be no "Jew and Gentile," "circumcision and uncircumcision," barbarian, Scythian, slave, freeman ; but CHRIST is ALL and everywhere.

12. Put on therefore, as the elect of God, holy and beloved, bowels of mercies, kindness, humbleness of mind, meekness, longsuffering ;

13. Forbearing one another, and forgiving one another, if any man have a quarrel against any : even as Christ forgave you, so also do ye.

14. And above all these things put on charity, which is the bond of perfectness.

15. And let the peace of God rule in your hearts, to the which also ye are called in one body ; and be ye thankful.

iii. 12-15. Put on then as the great God's chosen ones, holy, beloved, a tender, compassionate heart, lowliness, gentleness, patience under affront ; bearing with one another and forgiving one another, if any have a complaint against any. As the Lord has forgiven you, even so do you (forgive). To crown all put on love. That is the main tie of perfectness. And let the peace of God rule in your hearts, whereunto ye were called, one body all of you. Moreover, be thankful.

16. Let the word of Christ dwell in you richly in all wisdom ; teaching and admonishing one another in psalms and hymns and spiritual songs, singing with grace in your hearts to the Lord.

17. And whatsoever ye do in word or deed, do all in the name of the Lord Jesus, giving thanks to God and the Father by him.

iii. 16, 17. May Christ and His message dwell in you richly, and may you be altogether wise ! Teach one another and admonish one another, by God's good grace, with psalms, with hymns, with spiritual songs ; singing in your hearts to God. And anything you do, in word or in deed, let it be all in the Name of the Lord Jesus, with thanksgiving to God the Father through Him.

18. Wives, submit yourselves unto your own husbands, as it is fit in the Lord.

19. Husbands, love your wives, and be not bitter against them.

20. Children, obey your parents in all things : for this is well pleasing unto the Lord.

iii. 18-end. Wives, submit yourselves to your husbands as belongs to you "in the Lord."

Husbands, love your wives and be not ill-tempered towards them.

Children, obey your parents in everything, for this is commendable for a Christian.

| | |
|---|---|
| 21. Fathers, provoke not your children to anger, lest they be discouraged. | Fathers, do not irritate your children, that they may not lose heart. |
| 22. Servants, obey in all things your masters according to the flesh ; not with eyeservice, as menpleasers ; but in singleness of heart, fearing God : 23. And whatsoever ye do, do it heartily, as to the Lord, and not unto men ; 24. Knowing that of the Lord ye shall receive the reward of the inheritance : for ye serve the Lord Christ. 25. But he that doeth wrong shall receive for the wrong which he hath done : and there is no respect of persons. | Slaves, obey your earthly masters in everything, not with eyeservice as "manpleasers" but with absolute sincerity, from fear of the One Master. Whatever you are doing, work at it with heart and soul, as for the Lord and not for men ; being sure that from the Lord you shall receive the inheritance as your recompense. It is the Lord Christ Whose slaves you are. The wrong-doer, I say, shall receive the wrong he has done. There is no "favour" shown. |
| iv. 1. Masters, give unto your servants that which is just and equal ; knowing that ye also have a Master in heaven. | iv. 1. Masters, afford your slaves justice and fair treatment, being sure that you too have a Master in heaven. |
| 2. Continue in prayer, and watch in the same with thanksgiving ; 3. Withal praying also for us, that God would open unto us a door of utterance, to speak the mystery of Christ, for which I am also in bonds : 4. That I may make it manifest, as I ought to speak. | iv. 2-4. Pray steadily ; be wakeful when you pray ; be thankful also. Pray too for me, that God may open for me a door for the message, that I may tell of the "mystery" of Christ, which has made me a prisoner ; that I may make it plain, as I am bound to tell it. |
| 5. Walk in wisdom toward them that are without, redeeming the time. 6. Let your speech be alway with grace, seasoned with salt, that ye may know how ye ought to answer every man. | iv. 5, 6. Behave yourselves wisely in regard to those "outside." Use you opportunities, as they come. Let your discourse be always winning, agreeably seasoned, so that you may know (without the telling) how you ought to answer in every case. |
| 7. All my state shall Tychicus declare unto you, who is a beloved brother, and a faithful minister and fellowservant in the Lord : 8. Whom I have sent unto you for the same purpose, that he might know your estate, and comfort your hearts ; | iv. 7-9. All my concerns shall be made known to you by Tychicus, the beloved brother, and faithful minister and fellow-servant "in the Lord." Him I am sending to you for this very purpose, that you may get to know all about me, and that he |

9. With Onesimus, a faithful and beloved brother, who is one of you. They shall make known unto you all things which are done here.

10. Aristarchus my fellow-prisoner saluteth you, and Marcus, sister's son to Barnabas, (touching whom ye received commandments: if he come unto you, receive him;)

11. And Jesus, which is called Justus, who are of the circumcision. These only are my fellowworkers unto the kingdom of God, which have been a comfort unto me.

12. Epaphras, who is one of you, a servant of Christ, saluteth you, always labouring fervently for you in prayers, that ye may stand perfect and complete in all the will of God.

13. For I bear him record, that he hath a great zeal for you, and them that are in Laodicea, and them in Hierapolis.

14. Luke, the beloved physician, and Demas, greet you.

15. Salute the brethren which are in Laodicea, and Nymphas, and the church which is in his house.

16. And when this epistle is read among you, cause that it be read also in the church of the Laodiceans; and that ye likewise read the epistle from Laodicea.

17. And say to Archippus, Take heed to the ministry which thou hast received in the Lord, that thou fulfil it.

18. The salutation by the hand of me Paul. Remember my bonds. Grace be with you.

may comfort your hearts—and Onesimus the faithful and beloved brother, who is one of yourselves. They shall make known to you all the news of Rome.

iv. 10-14. Greeting to you from Aristarchus my fellow-prisoner, and from Mark the cousin of Barnabas, about whom you have received charges, "if he come to you, give him welcome"; and from Jesus, who is called Justus — men of the Circumcision.

These only join in the work of forwarding God's Kingdom. They have been to me a comfort.

Greeting to you from Epaphras, who is one of yourselves, a (true) servant of Jesus Christ, evermore wrestling on your behalf in his prayers that you may be established perfect and complete in all the Will of God. For I bear him witness that he is much concerned for you and for the folks at Laodicea and the folks at Hierapolis.

Greetings from Luke the beloved physician and from Demas.

iv. 15-18. Greet the brethren at Laodicea, and Nymphas and the "Church" that is in their house. And when the letter has been read before you, cause that it be read also in the assembly of the Laodiceans; and mind that you too read the Laodicean letter. Moreover, say to Archippus, Look to the ministry you have been delivered "in the Lord," that you discharge it aright.

The greeting is by the hand of me, Paul. Bear in mind my bonds. God's Grace be with you.

*Printed by* R. & R. CLARK, LIMITED, *Edinburgh.*

## 1981-82 TITLES

| No. | Author | Title | Price |
|---|---|---|---|
| 0102 | Blaikie, W. G. | Heroes of Israel | 19.50 |
| 0103 | Bush, George | Genesis (2 vol.) | 29.95 |
| 0202 | Bush, George | Exodus | 22.50 |
| 0302 | Bush, George | Leviticus | 10.50 |
| 0401 | Bush, George | Numbers | 17.75 |
| 0501 | Cumming, John | The Book of Deuteronomy | 16.00 |
| 0602 | Bush, George | Joshua & Judges (2 vol. in 1) | 17.95 |
| 2101 | MacDonald, James M. | The Book of Ecclesiastes | 15.50 |
| 2201 | Durham, James | An Exposition on the Song of Solomon | 17.25 |
| 2302 | Alexander, Joseph | Isaiah (2 vol.) | 29.95 |
| 3001 | Cripps, Richard S. | A Commentary on the Book of Amos | 13.50 |
| 3201 | Burns, Samuel C. | The Prophet Jonah | 11.25 |
| 4001 | Morison, James | The Gospel According to Matthew | 24.95 |
| 4102 | Morison, James | The Gospel According to Mark | 21.00 |
| 4403 | Stier, Rudolf E. | Words of the Apostles | 18.75 |
| 4502 | Moule, H. C. G. | The Epistle to the Romans | 16.25 |
| 4802 | Brown, John | An Exposition of the Epistle of Paul to the Galatians | 16.00 |
| 5102 | Westcott, F. B. | The Epistle to the Colossians | 7.50 |
| 5103 | Eadie, John | Colossians | 10.50 |
| 6201 | Lias, John J. | The First Epistle of John | 15.75 |
| 8602 | Shedd, W. G. T. | Theological Essays (2 vol. in 1) | 26.00 |
| 8603 | McIntosh, Hugh | Is Christ Infallible and the Bible True? | 27.00 |
| 9507 | Denney, James | The Death of Christ | 12.50 |
| 9508 | Farrar, F. W. | The Life of Christ | 24.95 |
| 9509 | Dalman, Gustav H. | The Words of Christ | 13.50 |
| 9510 | Andrews & Gifford | Man and the Incarnation & The Incarnation (2 vol. in 1) | 15.00 |
| 9511 | Baron, David | Types, Psalms and Prophecies | 14.00 |
| 9512 | Stier, Rudolf E. | Words of the Risen Christ | 8.25 |
| 9803 | Gilpin, Richard | Biblical Demonology: A Treatise on Satan's Temptations | 20.00 |
| 9804 | Andrews, S. J. | Christianity and Anti-Christianity in Their Final Conflict | 15.00 |

## TITLES CURRENTLY AVAILABLE

| | | | |
|---|---|---|---|
| 0101 | Delitzsch, Franz | A New Commentary on Genesis (2 vol.) | 27.75 |
| 0201 | Murphy, James G. | Commentary on the Book of Exodus | 12.75 |
| 0301 | Kellogg, Samuel H. | The Book of Leviticus | 19.00 |
| 0901 | Blaikie, William G. | The First Book of Samuel | 13.50 |
| 1001 | Blaikie, William G. | The Second Book of Samuel | 13.50 |
| 1101 | Farrar, F. W. | The First Book of Kings | 16.75 |
| 1201 | Farrar, F. W. | The Second Book of Kings | 16.75 |
| 1701 | Raleigh, Alexander | The Book of Esther | 9.00 |
| 1801 | Gibson, Edgar | The Book of Job | 9.75 |
| 1802 | Green, William H. | The Argument of the Book of Job Unfolded | 10.75 |
| 1901 | Dickson, David | A Commentary on the Psalms (2 vol.) | 29.25 |
| 1902 | MacLaren, Alexander | The Psalms (3 vol.) | 43.50 |
| 2001 | Wardlaw, Ralph | Book of Proverbs (2 vol.) | 29.95 |
| 2301 | Kelly, William | An Exposition of the Book of Isaiah | 13.25 |
| 2401 | Orelli, Hans C. von | The Prophecies of Jeremiah | 13.50 |
| 2601 | Fairbairn, Patrick | An Exposition of Ezekiel | 16.50 |
| 2701 | Pusey, Edward B. | Daniel the Prophet | 19.50 |
| 2702 | Tatford, Frederick | Daniel and His Prophecy | 8.25 |
| 3801 | Wright, Charles H. H. | Zechariah and His Prophecies | 21.95 |
| 4101 | Alexander, Joseph | Commentary on the Gospel of Mark | 15.25 |
| 4201 | Kelly, William | The Gospel of Luke | 16.95 |
| 4301 | Brown, John | The Intercessory Prayer of Our Lord Jesus Christ | 10.50 |
| 4302 | Hengstenberg, E. W. | Commentary on the Gospel of John (2 vol.) | 34.95 |
| 4401 | Alexander, Joseph | Commentary on the Acts of the Apostles (2 vol. in 1) | 27.50 |
| 4402 | Gloag, Paton J. | A Critical and Exegetical Commentary on Acts (2 vol.) | 27.50 |
| 4501 | Shedd, W. G. T. | Critical and Doctrinal Commentary on Romans | 15.75 |
| 4601 | Brown, John | The Resurrection of Life | 13.25 |
| 4602 | Edwards, Thomas C. | A Commentary on the First Epistle to the Corinthians | 16.25 |
| 4801 | Ramsay, William | Historical Commentary on the Epistle to the Galatians | 15.75 |
| 4901 | Westcott, Brooke, F. | St. Paul's Epistle to the Ephesians | 9.75 |
| 5001 | Johnstone, Robert | Lectures on the Book of Philippians | 16.50 |
| 5401 | Liddon, H. P. | The First Epistle to Timothy | 6.00 |
| 5601 | Taylor, Thomas | An Exposition of Titus | 17.50 |
| 5801 | Delitzsch, Franz | Commentary on the Epistle to the Hebrews (2 vol.) | 29.95 |
| 5802 | Bruce, A. B. | The Epistle to the Hebrews | 15.00 |
| 5901 | Johnstone, Robert | Lectures on the Epistle of James | 14.00 |
| 5902 | Mayor, Joseph B. | The Epistle of St. James | 19.25 |
| 6501 | Manton, Thomas | An Exposition of the Epistle of Jude | 12.00 |
| 6601 | Trench, Richard C. | Commentary on the Epistles to the Seven Churches | 8.50 |
| 7001 | Orelli, Hans C. von | The Twelve Minor Prophets | 13.50 |
| 7002 | Alford, Dean Henry | The Book of Genesis and Part of the Book of Exodus | 11.50 |
| 7003 | Marbury, Edward | Obadiah and Habakkuk | 21.50 |
| 7004 | Adeney, Walter | The Books of Ezra and Nehemiah | 11.50 |
| 7101 | Mayor, Joseph B. | The Epistle of St. Jude & The Second Epistle of Peter | 15.25 |
| 7102 | Lillie, John | Lectures on the First and Second Epistle of Peter | 18.25 |
| 7103 | Hort, F. J. A. & A. F. | Expository and Exegetical Studies | 29.50 |
| 7104 | Milligan, George | St. Paul's Epistles to the Thessalonians | 10.50 |
| 7105 | Stanley, Arthur P. | Epistles of Paul to the Corinthians | 20.95 |
| 7106 | Moule, H. C. G. | Colossian and Philemon Studies | 10.50 |
| 7107 | Fairbairn, Patrick | The Pastoral Epistles | 14.95 |
| 8001 | Fairweather, William | Background of the Gospels | 15.00 |
| 8002 | Fairweather, William | Background of the Epistles | 14.50 |
| 8003 | Zahn, Theodor | Introduction to the New Testament (3 vol.) | 48.00 |
| 8004 | Bernard, Thomas | The Progress of Doctrine in the New Testament | 9.00 |
| 8401 | Blaikie, William G. | David, King of Israel | 14.50 |
| 8402 | Farrar, F. W. | The Life and Work of St. Paul (2 vol.) | 43.95 |
| 8601 | Shedd, W. G. T. | Dogmatic Theology (4 vol.) | 49.50 |
| 8701 | Shedd, W. G. T. | History of Christian Doctrine (2 vol.) | 30.25 |
| 8702 | Oehler, Gustav | Theology of the Old Testament | 20.00 |
| 8703 | Kurtz, John Henry | Sacrificial Worship of the Old Testament | 15.00 |
| 8901 | Fawcett, John | Christ Precious to those that Believe | 9.25 |
| 9401 | Neal, Daniel | History of the Puritans (3 vol.) | 54.95 |
| 9402 | Warns, Johannes | Baptism | 11.50 |
| 9501 | Schilder, Klass | The Trilogy (3 vol.) | 48.00 |
| 9502 | Liddon, H. P. & Orr, J. | The Birth of Christ | 13.95 |
| 9503 | Bruce, A. B. | The Parables of Christ | 12.50 |
| 9504 | Bruce, A. B. | The Miracles of Christ | 17.25 |
| 9505 | Milligan, William | The Ascension of Christ | 12.50 |
| 9506 | Moule, H. C. & Orr, J. | The Resurrection of Christ | 16.95 |
| 9801 | Liddon, H. P. | The Divinity of our Lord | 20.25 |
| 9802 | Pink, Arthur W. | The Antichrist | 10.50 |
| 9803 | Shedd, W. G. T. | The Doctrine of Endless Punishment | 8.25 |

NOTES

# NOTES

# NOTES

NOTES

# NOTES